The Bible
and the Reader

AN INTRODUCTION TO LITERARY CRITICISM

Edgar V. McKnight

Fortress Press   **Philadelphia**

Library of Congress Cataloging in Publication Data

McKnight, Edgar V.
    The Bible and the reader.

    Includes index.
    1. Bible as literature.   2. Bible—Hermeneutics.
I. Title.
BS535.M35 1985   220.6′01   85–4603
ISBN 0–8006–1872–6

1733B85   Printed in the United States of America   1–1872

Contents

Acknowledgments

I owe a great debt to students and colleagues at Furman University who provide the challenge and support necessary for satisfying teaching and research. Assistance for this particular book has come through sabbatical leave and grants for travel and study from the administration and from university committees on research and faculty development. Participants in the 1984–86 "Project in Reading and Reader-Oriented Theories of Interpretation" sponsored at Furman by the National Endowment for the Humanities will recognize their influence on the book, as will colleagues in the Society for New Testament Studies and the Society of Biblical Literature who have participated in seminars over the past decade on "The Relevance of Linguistics and Semiotics for Exegesis," "Symbols, Metaphors and Models in the New Testament," and "Structuralism and Exegesis."

A special debt is owed to Professor Geoffrey Hartman of Yale University for the opportunity to participate in his 1980 NEH Summer Seminar on "Studies in Modern Literary Criticism."

The research for the book was begun during my 1981–82 tenure as Fulbright Senior Research Professor at the University of Tübingen, and the book is dedicated to Professor Peter Stuhlmacher of Tübingen's Theological Faculty and to participants in the *Sozietät* on *Erfahrung und Exegese* which Professor Stuhlmacher and I conducted in the fall semester of that year.

Introduction

This book may be read as a stage in my pilgrimage toward a method of biblical interpretation that is personally satisfying, meets requirements of intellectual honesty and critical rigor, and is faithful to theological concerns. The pilgrimage recounted here is not only personal, however; it is the quest of students of the Bible in general. The story is dynamic—it moves from a dogmatic context to historical and literary contexts.

DOGMATIC INTERPRETATION

The story begins for me in the churches I attended as a young person. What passages of the Bible I read or heard read were taken from here and there, the Old Testament or the New Testament, the letters of Paul or the Gospels—no matter. The context for selecting and reading the passages was the church.

This method has had a long and noble history; it was the method of the ancient and medieval church. Of course, in my limited situation, the context was not *the church:* it was a local congregation and a denomination, and the Bible was used to try to determine the answers to such questions as whether we ought to be allowed to go swimming on Sunday and whether playing cards was okay. It was used in debates between Methodists and Baptists on the question of "falling from grace."

A more comprehensive application of the dogmatic method may be illustrated through Augustine's interpretation of the parable of the Good

Samaritan, the story of a traveler who was robbed and beaten as he traveled from Jerusalem to Jericho. Although religious characters (a priest and a Levite) would not help the wounded man, a Samaritan (considered a half-breed by the religious establishment) befriended the poor man and provided for his care.

The story begins: "A man was going down from Jerusalem to Jericho, and he fell among robbers, who stripped him and beat him, and departed, leaving him half dead." Augustine interpreted the passage in this way:

> A certain man went down from Jerusalem to Jericho; Adam himself is meant; Jerusalem is the heavenly city of peace, from whose blessedness Adam fell; Jericho means the moon and signifies our mortality, because it is born, waxes, wanes, and dies. Thieves are the devil and his angels. Who stripped him, namely of his immortality; and beat him, by persuading him to sin; and left him half-dead, because in so far as man can understand and know God, he lives, but in so far as he is wasted and oppressed by sin, he is dead; he is therefore called half-dead. . . .[1]

Before he is through Augustine deals with such matters as the incarnation, the church, the second advent, and the practice of celibacy. The method is allegory, of course, but more important than the specific method is the context into which the material is being placed. Augustine made sense of the parable of the Good Samaritan by putting it into a churchly context, or perhaps more correctly by reading it in the light of his churchly context. Context is central in interpretation: the context in which we are situated and the context into which we fit the text. The two are really the same. As Jonathan Culler says: "To make sense of something is to bring it within a discursive order, to naturalize it or reduce its strangeness so that it speaks to us in an idiom we can understand."[2] Jacques Derrida says the same thing when he declares that "No meaning can be determined out of context." His additional statement is as important for biblical study as for the sort of literary study he favors: ". . . no context permits saturation."[3] The meaning of a text is inexhaustible because no context can provide us with the keys to all its possibilities.

1. Augustine, *Quaestiones Evangeliorum* II, 19. Cited in C. H. Dodd, *The Parables of the Kingdom*, 1.
2. Jonathan Culler, "Making Sense," 30.
3. Jacques Derrida, "Living On," 81.

Augustine placed the parable of the Good Samaritan in the context of the church and used allegory to reduce its strangeness. Augustine serves as an example, for he restated and impressed an earlier ecclesiastical system on the Middle Ages. For Augustine the task of interpretation required carefully revised texts, a clear concept of the content of the biblical canon, knowledge of the original biblical languages, and finally (and most important) the capacity to distinguish between the literal and the derived sense of scripture. His rule was that "whatever there is in the word of God that cannot, when taken literally, be referred to purity of life or soundness of doctrine, you may set down as figurative."[4] Purity of life is ethics. Soundness of doctrine is theology. Augustine used allegory to handle the fact that the context of the church does not permit saturation of all biblical texts.

The ancient and medieval method of reading the Bible in terms of the church's faith and ethics was satisfying in Augustine's day and in the religious communities of my high-school and college days. The ethical and theological earnestness was attractive. Great personal satisfaction was found in the life of a religious community that took the Bible seriously. I took the Bible seriously and tried to read it in light of all that I was leain high school and college. But the allegorical method was unacceptable to me when applied to biblical passages in which God told the Hebrews to slaughter all the inhabitants of Canaan or gave the Deuteronomic command that disobedient children be stoned to death by the elders of the city.

THE HISTORICAL-CRITICAL METHOD

In graduate school I discovered the historical-critical method of Bible study. This was an exhilarating discovery intellectually, emotionally, and spiritually. Instead of suiting the biblical text to a churchly system of knowledge and faith, the value of giving the texts their own historical weight was stressed. I learned that the Bible grew up out of the real experiences of real people and that the various parts of the Bible could be set in particular historical contexts.

---

4. Augustine, *On Christian Doctrine* Book III, x, 14.

Numerous historical and cultural factors were involved in the movement toward historical criticism. The Renaissance and the Reformation liberated Western culture from authority and tradition and allowed individuals to approach the Bible with reason. A rationalism developed which became a habit of thought for all people, including church people who came to test and communicate their beliefs by rational means.

The historical nature of the critical method was influenced by discoveries of geology and Darwinian evolutionary ideas. Under the influence of the evolutionary principle, the religion of the Bible came to be seen as a part of the sweep of history. Therefore, the meaning of the biblical documents was tied up with the historical context out of which they arose. The Bible came to be treated, therefore, as a collection of historical documents whose truth could not be understood apart from such matters as authorship, dating, circumstance of writing, and relationship with previous oral and written material.

The meaning of the parable of the Good Samaritan from the perspective of historical criticism was derived from the context of Jesus' proclamation of the kingdom in first-century Palestine. That meaning was determined by the historical and cultural situation of Jesus. Later an emphasis came to be placed not on the historical context of the events described but on the historical context of the writing of the documents. Instead of focusing on early first-century Palestine, the emphasis was on the Roman world of the later first century.

How could the biblical scholar in the church arrange and evaluate his or her findings with the view of history as an entire course of coherent and reciprocally related historical events—a view advanced by Ernst Troeltsch? History could be seen as the movement of the divine spirit itself and of events viewed in terms of universal historical progress. Historical criticism, then, enabled the believing critic to note the witness of the divine spirit in the historical witness of the scriptures or to see historical criticism as the method which allowed theology to share in and give shape to universal historical progress.

In our day, following on two bitter world wars and continuing social upheaval, it is rather difficult for history to be viewed as the upward moral development of humankind. We cannot easily mesh profane and divine history.

Rudolf Bultmann's existential interpretation must be mentioned here as an early response to the dilemma for interpretation posed by the European crisis of historical criticism. The question of the meaning of all history was replaced with the question of the individual's encounter with historic events and the theology of the Bible was limited to speaking in terms of human existence. Bultmann's approach was to look behind the biblical text to determine its existential content.

A NEW CONTEXT FOR INTERPRETATION

A historical model is no longer completely satisfying critically and theologically, for the assumptions that supported the approach are no longer compelling.

I became keenly aware of this disquieting state of affairs when I was asked to review a book by Erhardt Güttgemanns of the University of Bonn which had caused some stir in German New Testament circles. The title of the book was *Offene Fragen (Candid Questions)*, but it was more. It was a declaration that the whole tradition of New Testament scholarship had to be shelved. Historical criticism and existential interpretation were wrongheaded and had to be replaced by a linguistic exegesis. Form criticism was the first opponent to be demolished in Güttgemanns's work. Form criticism had emphasized the historical situation of the community as the matrix for the development of the forms of the Gospel narratives—forms such as parable, miracle story, and pronouncement story. Consider the pronouncement story. Form critics analyzed the narrative as a story in which Jesus is confronted with some question or problem; the climax of the story is a pronouncement by Jesus which was useful for preaching in the early church. An example is the story in which the Pharisees and Herodians try to trap Jesus with the question about paying taxes to the emperor. Jesus asks for a coin and indicates that the emperor's likeness is on the coin. "Render therefore to Caesar the things that are Caesar's, and to God the things that are God's" is the concluding statement. According to the form critics these stories developed in the church for preaching purposes. Güttgemanns said that history and the sociological situation of the early church had nothing to do with the essence of the forms. The forms on a deep level grow out of nonhistorical anthropomorphic and linguistic factors. When I was asked to review Güttgemanns's book for American readers, I was forced to rethink the whole set of assumptions and practices of historical criticism. Is the text, its form and meaning, the result of historical and cultural factors or of nonhistorical, transhistorical factors which might even govern the perception of history? I could not accept Güttgemanns's simplistic solution, but neither could I remain completely satisfied with my critical tradition.

As I see it now, there are several alternatives in our present situation.

1. We can continue the historical approach. Some will continue with the naive confidence of an earlier historicism. Others will use the method more cautiously but will see no other approach that is properly critical. I believe attempts to maintain or redefine historical method are doomed to failure because the historical method of criticism as such is no longer the prevailing model. We can no longer equate meaning with what the text meant and take what the text meant as the result, pure and simple, of its historical and cultural context.

2. We can give up the attempt to be critical and return to a precritical dogmatic approach. Much of the Bible can be read directly as statements about God and his will for humankind. But much of the Bible must simply be set aside when such an approach is used—if the Bible cannot be taken allegorically. If we are serious about studying the Bible with the full range of our rational faculties, however, we simply cannot retreat to a noncritical or precritical approach.

3. We can choose another study model. At one time, Güttgemanns encouraged us to reduce biblical material to the model of linguistics. The context for him was a text linguistics on the analogy of the sentence grammar of Noam Chomsky. But there are other models, other contexts, which we can employ. Sociology, various approaches in psychology, and economics can all be used as models or contexts for understanding the biblical text.

4. We can accept a number of these different models or contexts at the same time. We could examine the text as the result of historical and cultural forces. Then we could see the text as caused by anthropological and linguistic factors, explaining it as the result of a text grammar modeled on sentence grammar. Other reductions could take place as we applied various disciplines.

5. We can choose a literary approach as a productive way of

accommodating different models. The Bible is certainly literature. Most of it, indeed, is narrative, and the rules followed in the composition of the narrative are rules found in literary composition in general. When we took the narrative and forced it into a historical model as a literal account of the actual events being described, we had to perform some amazing feats. Take, for example, the simple matter of the cleansing of the temple in Jerusalem by Jesus. In the first three Gospels, the cleansing of the temple is placed toward the end of the ministry of Jesus. In the Gospel of John, however, the cleansing of the temple is placed at the beginning of Jesus' ministry. How can this be handled? Very simply, write a history of Jesus which includes two cleansings of the temple: one at the beginning of his ministry and another at the end. But when attention is given to the meaning of the temple, the significance of Jesus, and the relationship of Jesus to the temple *within the texts,* it becomes plain that confrontation is inevitable. In terms of plot, character, theme, and symbolism, there must be confrontation. Because the Synoptic writers see some development in the self-understanding of the Jesus of their story and follow a plot which does not have Jesus in Jerusalem until the final days, the confrontation must come at this point. John has no development— Jesus is the Word become flesh from the prologue on. Since John has Jesus in Jerusalem in the beginning of his career, confrontation must come early. A judgment is not being made as to the occurrence or non-occurrence of a confrontation. The critical judgment could be made that confrontation took place, that it took place late in Jesus' ministry, and that the significance of the confrontation in the Gospels is in agreement with the significance in the context of Jesus' ministry. I am suggesting, however, that we must begin with the material as a literary construction before we become concerned with history or theology.

The reader may protest that an illegitimate reduction of the biblical text is being attempted, that a literary context is being used instead of a dogmatic or historical or linguistic context but that the possible meaning of the text is being reduced by the literary context. This protest was probably valid in earlier periods of literary criticism. The fact that the biblical text was "practical" instead of "pure" literature made literary approaches problematic. Since the material had to do with theological values and was in some sense folk literature we were prevented from applying some of the dominant literary approaches. The literary criticism which is advocated, however, is not an early literary history or the criticism which attempts to bracket out (either theoretically or practically) anything not contained in the text itself. The literary approach which is seen as offering a new hope for biblical criticism has been spoken of as hermeneutic criticism. Advocates for and opponents of this newer method speak of criticism as entering into an "age of reading," because the reader is more deliberately included in the process of interpretation and analysis. Indeed, the definition of the ontological status of a work of literature includes the reader. The literary work is seen as existing within the triad of poet, text, and reader; the reality of a literary work is seen as essentially dependent upon its comprehension or realization by a reader. The inclusion of the reader in the work opens the text to a variety of values and meanings.[5]

Now that confidence in the historical method has begun to falter, we must move from this method to an inclusive literary-critical method which defines the literary work as including the reader. The kind of historical study we presently do in biblical studies is an incipient literary criticism, and an expansion of our present approach can result in a full-blown comprehensive approach to the biblical text as a literary phenomenon. In such an approach the model of interpretation would be changed from the quest for some meaning in the mind of the author to a meaning or a significance on this side of the text. Therefore, our goal is no longer a meaning *behind* the text which creates distance but rather a meaning *in front of* the text which demands involvement.

This book serves to introduce biblical readers and critics to theories and strategies in literary criticism which have been proposed and developed to enable readers to make sense of texts, a sense which is faithful and satisfying to both the text and the readers. Chapter 1 surveys

5. The theoretical basis for setting biblical study in the context of this newer literary criticism was given in my book *Meaning in Texts*. It shows that the hermeneutical concern for meaning is inevitably related to human linguistic processes and structures of concern in the structural tradition. There is a hermeneutical core at every structural level. In *Meaning in Texts*, I was primarily concerned with attempting to show how insights from structuralism could rehabilitate the hermeneutics in the tradition of Rudolf Bultmann. Hermeneutics needs the conceptualization of language in the tradition of Ferdinand de Saussure. For American and English scholars, Bultmann's existential approach was never really necessary or satisfying. We continued to have a naive confidence in the historical method even after postulates which supported that method had passed away.

the contours and convergences of literary criticism and biblical study to sensitize readers to the possibility of reading the Bible as literature. Chapters 2, 3, and 4 discuss the theories and strategies which promise assistance to readers who would find meaning for themselves in literature and in the Bible as literature. Chapter 5 provides a reader-oriented conceptualization of the role and function of literature which may accompany and make possible the use of the theories and strategies discussed in the earlier chapters.

CHAPTER 1

The Contours and Convergence of Biblical and Literary Criticism

Throughout history readers and critics from diverse perspectives have successfully applied various methods to make sense of the Bible. The ancient and medieval church's dogmatic approach with the allegorical method was an effective way in light of the Neoplatonic world view. The historical-critical and existential methods have proved their worth for post-Enlightenment readers. Today, biblical readers and critics are faced with new possibilities in the challenge to make sense in light of contemporary literary criticism and the world views supporting that criticism.

In the contemporary context, however, the chaotic field of critical theory itself must be tamed before criticism can be applied to biblical texts. We lack an established method of literary study that can bring about "assured results" of the sort possible with the historical approach. A growing number of biblical scholars view this situation positively because of the opportunity for creating approaches and interpretations to match the needs of contemporary readers and critics.

THE HISTORY AND PRINCIPLES OF LITERARY CRITICISM

Although contemporary literary criticism lacks one set of principles and methods that commands universal assent, some elements of literary study are recognized by literary critics in general. There is also a history of the different coordination of these elements which may help

1

contemporary readers and critics arrive at satisfying principles and methods.

The Coordinates of a Literary Work of Art

A useful way of charting the pattern of criticism is outlined by M. H. Abrams in *The Mirror and the Lamp*. The history and practice of criticism are illuminated by Abrams in terms of the dominance of one of the four elements in the comprehensive situation of a work of art: the work, the artist, the universe imitated in the work, and the audience.[1]

For the classical age, the mimetic orientation was characteristic, Plato and Aristotle being the great exponents of poetry as imitation. Horace's dictum that "the poet's aim is either to profit or to please, or to blend in one the delightful and the useful" united the classical theory of rhetoric (rhetoric being distinguished from poetics in Aristotle) with literary criticism, and pragmatic theories became dominant up through most of the eighteenth century. With romanticism, expressive theories developed, and the literary work of art was seen as the expression of the thought and feeling of the poet or it was defined in terms of the process of imagination that utilizes the images, thoughts, and feelings of the poet. Objective theories became dominant in the mid–twentieth century; the literary work became its own world that transcends the facts of composition, the imitated universe, the nature and character of the author, and the effect on the audience.[2]

The four elements of work, artist, imitated universe, and audience form a dynamic system of criticism in which each of the elements is a variable coordinate differing in meaning and function "according to the critical theory in which it occurs, the method of reasoning which the theorist characteristically uses, and the explicit or implicit world-view of which these theories are an integral part."[3] The challenge and the opportunity for criticism today is that no one of the elements is dominant. There is no single pervasive world view of which one theory could be an integral part and therefore which would be dominant in literary criticism. All of the elements whirl in combinations which defy simple systemization.

1. M. H. Abrams, *The Mirror and the Lamp*.
2. Ibid., 8–29.
3. Ibid., 7.

Criticism and History

In the mid–twentieth century, the work of art itself was seen as transcending the other elements. In fact, Abrams suggests that while theories centering on the imitated universe, the audience, and the artist explore the work of art in relation to those elements, the theories centering upon the work of art "will explain the work by considering it in isolation, as an autonomous whole, whose significance and value are determined without any reference beyond itself."[4]

The beginning of the movement in America which resulted in the dominance of objective theories of literary criticism was a protest of literary scholars against the negation or at least the containment of literary criticism by literary history. In his championing of a new criticism in the 1930s, R. S. Crane drew a sharp distinction between literary history and literary criticism. Literary criticism is understood by Crane as "any reasoned discourse concerning works of imaginative literature the statements in which are primarily statements about the works themselves and appropriate to their character as productions of art." The understanding with which criticism is concerned is not equivalent to "knowing why an author said what he said (in a genetic or historical sense)." Rather it is equivalent to "knowing what it is he is saying and his reasons for saying it (in the sense of its artistic rationale)."[5]

Crane was very negative in his evaluation of the contribution which literary history makes to literary criticism. He declared:

> If literary criticism is what we want, very little of "the great body of purely genetic and historical investigations which have absorbed the energies of so many professors of literature and the results of which have formed the content of so many courses in our colleges and universities" is germane.[6]

As a fundamental prerequisite of criticism, literary history is boldly dismissed: "of literary history as such, in its distinctly genetic and narrative aspects, there is seldom need to take account."[7]

In the 1940s René Wellek said that theory, history, and criticism, "implicate each other so thoroughly" as to make one inconceivable

4. Ibid.
5. R. S. Crane, *The Idea of the Humanities and Other Essays*, 11, 16.
6. Ibid., 17.
7. Ibid., 17–18.

without the others. But he also saw a type of literary history which would practically deny the need for genuine literary criticism. Such history sees itself as dealing with verifiable facts and using standards of the past. It does not need the opinions and judgments of contemporary critics. Such history or historical reconstruction comes to center on the intention of the author. "It is usually assumed that if we can ascertain this intention and can see that the author has fulfilled it, we can also dispose of the problem of criticism. The author has served a contemporary purpose and there is no need or even possibility of further criticizing his work."[8]

After the victory of criticism and the dominance of the New Criticism, Crane spoke in 1957 of his own activities as "rhetorical shock tactics" and lamented that the New Criticism not only revolted "against the limitations of the older learning" but also "against the very conception of intellectual method that gave it its status as a learning."[9] Crane's belated hope might give direction to biblical critics who are stressing the need for genuine literary criticism of biblical texts:

> There was little reason, once the friends of criticism had got a hearing, why they should not help to reconstruct university literary studies in a spirit of conservative reform: carrying on the reinvigorating of the philological and historical tradition, and at the same time, and in this context, developing what that tradition had been relatively weak in—systematic training in the various modes of critical analysis and judgment.[10]

In a 1963 response to attacks against the New Criticism, Wellek strongly urged that the emphasis of New Criticism upon the literary work of art as "a verbal structure of a certain coherence and wholeness" did not and could not be conceived to mean "a denial of the relevance of historical information for the business of poetic interpretation."[11] The challenge of Wellek—to conceive of the literary work of art as related to external factors such as history and society—is not only a challenge to the New Criticism. It is also a challenge to more recent structural views of and approaches to literary texts. Can we organize the coordinates of literary study in a fashion to do justice to the literary work while relating

---

8. René Wellek and Austin Warren, *Theory of Literature*, 30, 33.

9. Crane, *Idea of Humanities*, 26.

10. Ibid., 26–27.

11. René Wellek, *Concepts of Criticism*, 7.

the work to external historical, social, and psychological factors with their own sets of relationships?

Hermeneutic Criticism

Traditional literary criticism has stressed that criticism is "reasoned discourse" and "intellectual method." The direct sensory and imaginative appreciation of literary works has not been seen as criticism, although such appreciation is a necessary condition and an important consequence of criticism. The presupposition of traditional literary criticism as to the relationship of appreciation, enjoyment, and understanding to the critical task has been called into question by hermeneutics, which emphasizes that a text has meaning only in relation to its interpreter. The growth of the importance of "understanding" for criticism has implications for the autotelic view of the literary work of art.

Edgar Lohner reflects the new turn in criticism with the question: "How can a critic communicate, in terms that are universally valid, the result of an act of comprehension which can be realized only individually and subjectively?"[12] Lohner reconciles the claims for the autonomy of the literary work with claims for the cognitive value of the work by a definition of the ontological status of a work of art which includes the reader. He affirms that "the literary work of art exists essentially within the triad of poet, work, and reader" and that the literary work of art "forever remains essentially dependent upon its comprehension by a reader."[13] Because the work of art involves the reader, criticism must ask about the mind of the reader and about the nature of the act resulting in the literary work of art and the process of understanding.

The criticism which includes the insights of poetics and which may be seen as the proper heir of New Criticism is termed "revisionist" or "hermeneutic" criticism by Geoffrey Hartman. It is defined in terms of its major characteristic of inclusiveness as contrasted with the exclusive tendency of the New Criticism. In retrospect, Hartman says, the New Criticism's insistence on the autonomy of the literary work and even the autonomy of criticism itself may be seen as an Anglo-American

---

12. Edgar Lohner, "The Intrinsic Method: Some Reconsiderations," 170.
13. Ibid., 170, 168.

"prejudice against mixing art with anything, especially with philosophy."[14] The revisionists, in contrast to the New Criticism, throw open the doors to "foreign elements" imported from across the Atlantic and from philosophy, theology, linguistics, sociology, and psychoanalysis. These revisionists have a "methodological faith" that "thinking and writing, criticism and literature, art and philosophy are creative modes to be worked through in tandem or in concert."[15] The genuinely different task foreseen by revisionism is the hermeneutic one: "to understand understanding through the detour of the writing/reading experience."[16]

In forsaking the straight line (the "stigmatic approach") and seeing the detour (the "wilderness full of ambivalent symbols and indirect signs")[17] as the appropriate hermeneutic path, revisionism criticizes genealogical or historical reasoning and emphasizes the role of formal genres. Two other recurrent issues involved in the hermeneutic detour have to do with relationships between factors often separated in traditional literary criticism. The creative and critical, which seem to be marginal to each other, are viewed as interdependent and central in their relationship to hermeneutic criticism. "To an extent," Hartman declares, "what is involved is the right to one's own tongue. We want to have our say despite or within authoritative pressures."[18]

The literary structuralism founded on the structural linguistics of Ferdinand de Saussure is cited by Hartman as helping provide the impetus for criticism to cross geographical and disciplinary lines. In the linguistics of Saussure, elements are defined by relationships, identities, and differences. Two major types of relationships are syntagmatic and paradigmatic (or associative). The linear sequence of signs in actual discourse forms a syntagmatic relationship. In this relationship a term acquires value because it stands in opposition to other words in the discourse. There is a syntagmatic relationship between "James" and "runs" which allows the sentence "James runs." This relationship exists between any two words, the first of which can serve as subject to the second. Syntagmatic relationships serve to help define a word in that the

14. Geoffrey Hartman, "Literary Criticism and Its Discontents," 213.
15. Ibid., 214.
16. Ibid., 216.
17. Ibid.
18. Ibid., 216, 217.

differences between a word and the other words in an acceptable sentence are crucial in the definition of the word. Non-syntagmatic relationships of signs are also essential. Saussure uses the term "associative" to refer to one set of non-syntagmatic relationships. He says that words which have something in common are associated in memory. For example, the word "teaching" will unconsciously call to mind numerous other words: "teach," "acquaint," "education," "apprenticeship," and other terms related to these words. All of these relationships are essential in the sense that a word loses its old identity when it loses some such relationships and gains others. For example, if there were not a word "education," the word "teaching" would change its identity in a subtle way. A different approach to non-syntagmatic relationships is taken by Saussure in his discussion of sentence construction and sentence interpretation. Paradigmatic relationships of a word are those that it has with words which may replace it in a sentence without making the sentence unacceptable. In the sentence "James runs," the verb "run" may be replaced by numerous other verbs such as "move," "flee," and "hasten." Again, all the paradigmatic relationships of a word (all the words which could be used in place of "runs") are essential in determining the formal identity of the word.

Syntagmatic and paradigmatic relationships have been illustrated in terms of words and sentences. Saussure claims, however, that the entire linguistic system can be reduced to a theory of syntagmatic and paradigmatic relations. When this view is accompanied by the view that literature and other aspects of culture are levels of language, the rationale is provided for literary criticism's crossing of all previously determined limits.

In hermeneutic criticism, structuralism is not taken as the means for a "supreme synthesis" or a "final knowledge" (although a first wave of literary structuralists saw in Saussure the hope for a solid scientific base for criticism). Nor is structuralism taken as an argument against the possibility of any knowledge (although a later wave sees such a consequence in the conception of Saussure). Structuralism, or structural semiotics (which sees language as only one semiotic system to be considered along with others in providing a more inclusive semiotics) provides the basis for a "unified field" theory of criticism—modeled on the human world—in which meaning is finally human and is determined by the reader in relation to the text. The structural-semiotic approach provides a proper place for the text as a statement of the literary past and for the contemporary reader-critic in the creation of meaning.

A LITERARY-ORIENTED BIBLICAL CRITICISM

A literary approach to the Bible has grown logically out of the recent history of biblical criticism. This section shows how literary criticism may be grafted onto the historical approach and how a reader-oriented perspective may allow the Bible to become genuine literature.

A New Situation in Biblical Criticism

The critical method of Bible study which arose in the eighteenth century was concerned with knowledge and understanding that could be authenticated by the presuppositions and methods of the Enlightenment. Rationalism, along with the revolutionary discoveries of geology and Darwinian evolutionary ideas, influenced the development of the historical-critical method. Today, however, the historical confidence or "historicism" that sees the locus of meaning in history is no longer dominant. Moreover, careful attention to the nature of the biblical text has caused scholars to see the necessity of genuine literary criticism to complete the historical task. For example, the narratives telling the story of Israel and the early Christian movement have been treated in succession as historical accounts of the events they depict, as collections of traditions reflecting the history of the communities that originated and transmitted them, and as documents reflecting the period in which they were composed. Contemporary redaction criticism is concerned with studying the theological motivation of an author as this is revealed in the use of traditional material to compose new material and new forms. After a quarter century of massive research using redactional-critical assumptions, Norman Perrin declared that conventional redaction criticism was no longer adequate because "it defines the literary activity of the Evangelist too narrowly." Not only is the full range of literary activity of the author missed, but serious injustice is also done "to the text of the Gospel as a coherent text with its own internal dynamics."[19] Historical criticism needs literary criticism to complete its task. But literary criticism is changing the historical approach which gave it birth.

Bultmann's Existential Approach

Long before contemporary developments in redaction criticism, Rudolf Bultmann had approached literary criticism in his use of existential categories to interpret the New Testament. Bultmann began not with traditional literary principles and methods but with poetics, the way that the mind creates story. This sort of approach was set in motion for Bultmann by Hans Jonas who saw the mind as symbolistic—interpreting itself in objective formula and symbols. Since the mind takes a detour by the symbol, the original phenomena hidden in the symbolic camouflage can be reached only through a long procedure of working back to the demythologized consciousness. Although Martin Heidegger's categories are used to explicate what Bultmann sees as the genuine subject matter of the New Testament, it is in the work of Jonas that a justification for demythologizing was found.[20]

A literary approach that would attempt to relate itself to the efforts of Bultmann (and to the New Hermeneutic which continued his efforts) must see the limitations of Bultmann's approach. Bultmann's program of scientific investigation seeks to convey some intellectual content and is therefore not inclusive enough to embrace the full range of literary meanings and language functions. The biblical text may be taken to refer to human existence, but there are functions alongside the referential (or cognitive). These include the emotive, conative, poetic, phatic, and metalingual functions (to use the categories of Jakobson). The full range of meanings that can be obtained through literary approaches must be appreciated by the biblical critic.

Reading the Bible as Literature

The reorientation of the critical task whereby the reader-critic is seen as inextricably involved with the text in the creation of meaning gives criticism a new perspective on traditional questions such as "what is

19. Norman Perrin, "The Interpretation of the Gospel of Mark," 120.
20. James M. Robinson, "Hermeneutics Since Barth," 34–37.

literature?" and allows the rapprochement of literary criticism and biblical study. Literature is what we read as literature. Instead of attempting to define the Bible as literature according to descriptive and historical criteria, we read the Bible as literature.

What does it mean to read the Bible as literature? Are we to deny that biblical texts grew out of specific historical and theological contexts and were designed to satisfy particular needs in those contexts? Original use is not denied, even though it must be observed that the moment after the text was received by the first readers the limited original use was exhausted. The text began to be read differently almost immediately after its initial reception, even by the first readers. And readers who were not original recipients of the text made sense in their own contexts with their different needs. Our reconceptualizing of biblical texts as literature follows the pattern implicitly followed by readers from the earliest days.

How is it possible to conceptualize as literature those biblical texts that originally had specific historical purposes? The distinction made by Aristotle between literature and history provides a starting point:

> It is not the poet's business to relate actual events, but such things as might or could happen in accordance with probability or necessity. A poet differs from a historian, not because one writes verse and the other prose . . . , but because the historian relates what happened, the poet what might happen. That is why poetry is more akin to philosophy and is a better thing than history; poetry deals with general truths, history with specific events.[21]

Aristotle's distinctions between history and literature may be restated from the reader's perspective and may help the process of translating biblical texts into literature. To read a text as history is to read it as a specific event, as what happened to particular individuals in geographically and temporally limited contexts. To read a text as literature is to read it as a universal truth.

The literary approach not only moves to the more universal so as to be able to be relevant to contemporary readers, it also gives more attention to the linguistic and literary materials used. The historical reduction emphasizes what is said rather than the way it is said; a literary approach places emphasis upon the style and form of what is said.

21. Aristotle, *The Poetics*, chap. 9.

Biblical critics are so accustomed to the historical reduction that a conscious volitional act may be necessary to change the focus from the historical (or theological) to the literary. Edward Gibbon's *Decline and Fall of the Roman Empire* illustrates helpfully how a work that was originally intended to be history has become literature. As Northrop Frye states:

> In the first place, Gibbon's work survives by its "style," which means that it insensibly moves over from the historical category into the poetic, and becomes a classic of English literature, or at any rate of English cultural history. In proportion as it does so, its material becomes universalized: it becomes an eloquent and witty meditation on human decline and fall, as exemplified by what happened in Caesarian Rome. The shift in attention is simultaneously from the particular to the universal and from what Gibbon says to his way of saying it. We read him for his "style" in the sense that the stylizing or conventionalizing aspect of his writing gradually becomes more important than the representational aspect.[22]

Frye is describing what has happened in the history of reception of Gibbon's work, of course. But what has happened in the course of history may also take place in the conscious choice of individual readers. The reader may choose to place biblical writing in a literary frame, emphasizing the style and the universal signification so as to enable him- or herself to create world and self both affectively and cognitively through interaction with the text.

History in Literary Study of the Bible

Attention to the original situation of communication does not abolish the work as literature if the total range of meanings and meaning-effects impinging upon the author and reader is considered, if unconscious and implicit meanings are allowed, and if these meanings are not held to apply only in the original situation. The biblical critic, trained as a historian, might find it satisfying and appropriate to continue to use the historical model, giving attention to the original situation of the text but expanding the concept of "meaning of the text" to include the totality of meanings and meaning-effects which impinge upon humankind. As biblical scholars integrate the literary approaches they find satisfying,

22. Northrop Frye, *The Great Code*, 46–47.

the original situation may be understood and appreciated more fully. The text will be read as literature in a more comprehensive way. Past and present coalesce, as do thematic content and structure. Continuity may be assumed between the cognitive and affective meaning and meaning-effect; continuity may also be assumed between the original meaning intended by the author, unconscious and implicit meanings of the author, and contemporary meaning-for-the-reader.

Biblical critics are discovering that it is possible to make sense out of literary criticism, to develop literary approaches to biblical texts which, while not completely objective and scientific, are orderly and rational. The literary approaches dissolve the distance between the ancient texts and the modern reader-critic. Such approaches do not depend upon an unacceptable historicism for justification, yet they allow for integration of the rich resources of the historical-critical tradition.

Postmodernism and Biblical Interpretation

At the same time that the values of literary criticism for biblical interpretation are becoming evident, however, criticism and interpretation are becoming problematic. Contemporary literary criticism, in fact, may be seen as the conflict between modern and postmodern philosophies and strategies. "Modern" here refers to ideas related to metaphysical and philosophical developments going back to Descartes. The capacity of the human subject to analyze critically and scientifically the literary object is presupposed. "Postmodernism" emphasizes the end of that sort of human rationality by denying Cartesian assumptions about human being (the subject), the world (object), the rational process, and truth. In contemporary forms of postmodernism and poststructuralism (deconstruction), the linguistics of Saussure is used (particularly as it was interpreted in French structuralism) as a model to emphasize the differential nature of meaning and the impossibility of discovery by the subject of some primitive or final meaning.

The thesis of this book is that readers make sense. Even if the subject making sense is not autonomous, and even if the sense is not some final synthesis of meaning, a meaning is discovered or created that is satisfying for the present location of the reader.

Structuralism is central for understanding the situation of contemporary critical thought. The structuralism which is emphasized is not the French variety that developed in opposition to existentialism. The whole of culture is not reduced to the formal codes of structuralism. Claude Lévi-Strauss's reduction of meaning and the human being to binary oppositions is not taken as a given because human beings and cultural achievements are not viewed as reducible to the world of which humanity is a part. The theoretical background against which contemporary developments are seen, then, is the formalist-structuralist-semiotic tradition that began with the structural conceptualization of the literary work as an organized whole, but that quickly accommodated cultural codes and the specific set or attitude of the individual subject to the structural conceptualization.

The problems and alternatives facing literary criticism are to be seen clearly in the American context which is a strategic battleground of literary theory. The way out of the critical impasse will involve an appropriation from earlier studies in the structural tradition which, up to the present, have played only an indirect part on the American scene. Chapter 2, therefore, will be devoted to the theoretical backgrounds of reader-oriented literary criticism (the formalist-structuralist-semiotic tradition)—a background which provides valuable views of the ways that the structures of the literary work may be related to cultural codes and to the individual reader in the process of actualization or concretization by the reader. In chapter 3 specific European contributions to literary criticism as a method of reader interaction with the text will be explicated. French structuralism will be examined as one of these contributions. The ideology of French structuralism is thereby neutralized but its positive contributions are delineated and utilized. The reader will then be prepared for chapter 4 which discusses the American context of literary criticism. The concluding chapter will deal with the reconceptualization of the role and function of literature (including biblical literature) which must accompany the reader-oriented strategies discussed in the preceding three chapters if those strategies are to be appropriated in current literary study.

CHAPTER 2

The Formalist-Structuralist Tradition

The major background for contemporary scholarly interest in the activity of the reader is the formalist-structuralist tradition. This may come as a surprise to many, for the reputation of structuralism is that of an approach in which neither historicity nor individual valuative reaction plays a role. The structuralism that became the vogue in the 1960s, indeed, was a French version that attempted to trace texts back to ahistorical abstract structures, and no place was made for the historical individuality of the reader or of the text itself.

Formal and structural approaches to literature grew out of the structural linguistics of Ferdinand de Saussure, and in an early phase of formalism, the Moscow linguistic circle (notably Roman Jakobson) regarded poetics as an integral part of linguistics and took the position that "a scientific poetics becomes possible only when it foregoes all valuation."[1] Nevertheless, Viktor Sklovskij, a representative of the Leningrad branch known as the Society for the Study of Poetic Language, observed that an author can compose a nonliterary writing that is perceived as literary and a literary piece which is perceived as nonliterary, and concluded that "artistry . . . results from what kind of perception we have."[2] From the beginning, therefore, a radical structuralist position was not unanimously maintained.

1. Roman Jakobson, "Die neueste russische Poesie," 23. Quoted in D. W. Fokkema and Elrud Kunne-Ibsch, *Theories of Literature in the Twentieth Century*, 185 n. 2.
2. Viktor Sklovskij, "Die Kunst als Verfahren," 7. Quoted in Fokkema and Kunne-Ibsch, *Theories of Literature*, 185 n. 2.

RUSSIAN FORMALISM

Structure and the Reader

By the late 1920s, Russian formalism as a whole had moved away from a one-sided linguistic approach to literature and had become interested in semantics and literary history. Nevertheless, the way formalists conceptualized the reader's interaction with the writing was influenced by their structural view of the work. A literary work was seen as an organized whole, made up of factors of varying importance with the semantic function nearly always having at least a minor role. The philosopher Gustav Spet, whose work on structuralism was known to the Russian formalists, had stressed that the various parts of a structure function in relation to context and the specific set or attitude of the observer. All parts of a structure, then, are potentially effective, implicit forms becoming explicit in relation to the context and attitude of the observer.[3] Essays of Sergej Bernstejn and Jurij Tynjanov reflect this perspective and stress not only the wholeness of the work of art but also the necessity of treating the reception of literature as a subject of research.

Sergej Bernstejn

In 1927 Bernstejn wrote an essay on "Aesthetic Presuppositions of a Theory of Recitation" that distinguishes between the text or the material object and the aesthetic object constituted by the reader on the basis of the text. The written poem is the work of art and the oral recitation of the poem is the aesthetic object. In oral composition (recitation) the aesthetic object is realized in some ways not dictated by the written form.

The basic factors of the artistic structure are material and form, and they are interdependent. The word made up of phonemes serves as the material of poetry. The written word itself, however, contains different possibilities, and choices must be made in the actual recitation. The written word of the poem, then, may be realized in the recitation in different ways depending upon the accent given—the intensity, the duration, and the pitch given to phonemes. In recitation, emotional coloring is given in part by discovering and concretizing tendencies of

---

3. Fokkema and Kunne-Ibsch, *Theories of Literature*, 20–22.

the poem itself and in part by the introduction of something new. "The factors of composition provided by the recitation—tempo, melody, strength of voice, articulation—have a necessary effect on the emotional level."[4] Bernstejn concludes that the written poem is characterized by immateriality, abstractness, and plurality of meaning. In the recitation, however, on the basis of the possibilities offered in the written poem, we find complete material precision and relatively univocal meaning.

Since the work of art is seen as a unified structure, the study of the work and the constitution of the aesthetic object is not a matter of an analysis of individual elements but a matter of the definition of points of view which the object allows. The totality of the points of view required by the object defines its structure, and the aesthetic object is formed through these points of view. The importance of the point of view in structural analysis is illustrated by a work that was not originally a literary work of art. The *Chronicle of Nestor* (a most important early authority for Russian history in the form of annals from the period A.D. 850–1110) can be read as three different objects: historical source, literary work, or a monument of language. The general point of view that defines the object determines the point of view which results in structural analysis. When the *Chronicle of Nestor* is seen as a monument of language, for example, the structures will be appropriately subordinated to that sort of object—sound, morphology, syntax, lexicography, and semiology.[5]

Jurij Tynjanov

Tynjanov provided a conceptualization of literature that related the structural concept to literary evolution and to nonliterary realities. Tynjanov viewed literature as a series and a system that stands in correlation with other series and systems and is defined through this correlation. Elements are not only correlated with other elements in the same literary system, they are correlated with other systems. Moreover, systems of literature are correlated with nonliterary systems. The vocabulary of a particular work, for example, is in correlation with

4. Sergej Bernstejn, "Ästhetische Voraussetzungen einer Theorie der Deklamation," 383, 385.
5. Ibid., 347.

literary and nonliterary vocabulary in general and with nonvocabulary elements in the same work.

The material of literature takes different forms at different periods of development because different principles of construction are operative. Tynjanov suggests a cycle of literary evolution that begins with a period of equilibrium or with an automatized principle of construction: in a dialectical relationship to the automatized principle of construction, a competing principle of construction announces itself; as the competing principle begins to grow, it seeks the easiest possibility of application; as the new principle becomes more powerful, it is extended to the largest possible number of phenomena; finally, the new principle is automatized and a competing principle of construction comes into being.[6]

Tynjanov applies this insight to the matter of genre. New genres are noted in confrontation with traditional genres. The new genres are not developments of the old, but replacements of the old. In the period of its decay, a genre moves from the center of critical attention to the populai periphery of literature. The new genre comes from the hitherto insignificant areas of literature. Tynjanov suggests that the genre of "adventure story" had moved to the center and then to the periphery when the genre "psychological novel" took its place. In Tynjanov's day, the psychological novel was becoming a popular genre on the periphery of genuine literary interest.[7]

In a discussion of the literary evolution of the letter genre, Tynjanov shows how nonliterary and literary forms become interrelated. In the first half of the eighteenth century, the letter was not part of literary life. Not prose, but poetry, the high ode, was dominant; and all doors were closed to the letter as a literary genre. It was only when small prose forms began to threaten the poetic genre that the possibility for a literary view of the letter arose. The way this came about is somewhat complicated. The principle of construction in the eighteenth century centered in oratorical speech. The oratorical and emotionally stimulating poetic word was important. Later, however, oratorical speech was replaced by the romance of the song. With this change, small forms and emotions came to the foreground. These were found useful because of the new

6. Jurij Tynjanov, "Das Literarische Faktum," 411–13.
7. Ibid., 397–401.

principle of construction. It was in this connection that the letter was able to enter the field of literature. "Here in the letters were found . . . phenomena which the new principle of construction was able to feature with extraordinary power: the incomplete speaking, the fragmentary, the allusions and 'domestic' small form of the letter motivated the introduction of trifles and such stylistic methods as were opposed to the 'elevated' methods of the eighteenth century."[8] So, the nonliterary document came to the center of literary interest and the letter came to be read not only by its original recipients in light of its message or statement but by later readers as a literary work.

Tynjanov's emphasis is not upon the activity of the reader in the structuring process. The reader is not seen as consciously considering and choosing various possibilities in the constructions and deconstructions involved in literary evolution. The perception of genre, for example, is not dependent upon the arbitrariness of the receiver, but upon the actual presence of a definite genre.[9] Individual and social influences may play a part in the modification and deformation of literature, however, and they must be clarified in the totality of relationships, not in a directly causal fashion. The method of Tynjanov is in contrast to "the establishment of the direct 'influence' " of major social factors that replaces the study of the *evolution* of literature with the study of the modifications of literary works—that is to say, of their deformation."[10]

JAN MUKAROVSKY: CZECH STRUCTURALISM

The relationship of the organization and structure of the literary work of art to social factors and to the individual subject's contribution to the literary process is a question that is debated vigorously today. The current debate can benefit from Mukarovsky's attempt to apply structural insights in literary study, an attempt that realized the need to move beyond the intrinsic organization of linguistic and literary elements

8. Ibid., 419.
9. Ibid., 397.
10. Jurij Tynjanov, "On Literary Evolution," 77.

to social and individual factors. The work of Mukarovsky may be divided into three stages. In the first stage, Mukarovsky's concern was the organization of the work and distinction between art and nonart on the basis of organization. The second stage moved to concern with the relation of art to the aesthetic code and the relationship between the aesthetic code and other codes. This stage emphasized social constraints. A third stage gave attention to the role the subject plays in the aesthetic process.

The Organization of the Work of Art

In the period from 1928 to 1934, Mukarovsky's structural analysis emphasized the material aspect of the work of art. The purpose of his detailed analysis of a poetic text of the period, *Macha's May: An Aesthetic Study* (1928), was to "discover the skeleton which provided the changeable stream of sounds with a firm outline."[11] The following year in a lecture entitled "On Contemporary Poetics," Mukarovsky defined the purpose of structural analysis as "discovering in the work those features which cause its aesthetic efficacy."[12] For Mukarovsky it was the organization that caused an object to be aesthetically effective. Mukarovsky's early concentration on the internal organization of the work of art echoed Tynjanov's dialectic concept of artistic forms involving struggle for dominance among the components of the work of art. The intrinsic organization of elements is contradictory. This causes the mutual subordination and superordination of elements to be in constant flux. Mukarovsky used the concept of "deautomatization" to explain the aesthetic effect of art.

In Mukarovsky's use, "deautomatization" referred to the separation of literary works from the automatized context of ordinary life by their peculiar organization. Within the work of art, one element or group of elements becomes dominant, and all the other elements are subordinated to the needs of the dominant. Every aesthetic deautomatization has two features: consistency and systematization.

> The work is consistent in that its deautomatized element is transformed throughout the work in a fixed manner. . . . The systematic character of

11. Quoted in Peter Steiner, "Jan Mukarovsky's Structural Aesthetics," xiii.
12. Ibid., xiv.

deautomatization on the other hand rests in the hierarchy of interrelations among its elements; i.e., the elements are subordinated and superordinated to each other. The element which stands the highest in this hierarchy is the dominant. All the other elements and their relations, whether deautomatized or automatized, are evaluated from the standpoint of this dominant.[13]

Social Codes

The activities of Mukarovsky after 1934 gave specific attention to the aesthetic norms or codes that constrain aesthetic interaction between a subject and an object. The subject was something of a passive vehicle of the supra-individual structure. The key Mukarovsky used to move from a one-sided orientation favoring the material aspect of art to social awareness and the set of norms valid for a particular collectivity was the category of *sign*. The meaning and signification of the organization of the work of art and not simply the organization itself became important. The work of art as a sign must consider the code that makes the work of art a social fact. Human culture is seen as a network of codes such as those of art, science, and religion. A particular code is defined according to its dominant function that groups objects together. But the products of human activity are polyfunctional; they may be organized by different codes. The codes themselves coexist and interact as society develops. The sign, then, cannot be analyzed completely without taking account of the code of a given linguistic group. The aesthetic code is the background against which the organization of the work of art is perceived and determines the actual appearance of the work.

In 1934, Mukarovsky presented his concept of the semiotics of art in an address before the Eighth International Congress of Philosophy in Prague. In his address, Mukarovsky explicated the character of the work of art as a sign. As a sign, the work of art is not to be identified with the "work-thing" (the sensory symbol created by the author). It is not even to be identified with the individual state of consciousness of its author or of any of its perceiving subjects. In Mukarovsky's view, the aesthetic object is related to the individual state of consciousness evoked by the work-thing only through what is common to all of the individual states of consciousness. "The work-thing functions . . . only as an external symbol . . . to which corresponds in the social consciousness a

13. Ibid.

meaning . . . consisting of what the subjective states of consciousness evoked in the members of a certain collectivity have in common."[14] The "aesthetic object" is the meaning in the consciousness of the particular collectivity.

In a study culminating the second state of Mukarovsky's structuralist aesthetic, "Aesthetic Function, Norm and Value as Social Facts," Mukarovsky explained how the work of art may be responsible for different aesthetic objects. This dynamic nature of the work of art helps us understand its function.

> The work of art itself is not a constant. Every shift in time, space or social surroundings alters the existing artistic tradition through whose prism the art work is observed, and as a result of such shifts that aesthetic object also changes which in the awareness of a member of a particular collective corresponds to a material artifact—an artistic product.[15]

The changeability of aesthetic evaluation, then, is not a secondary phenomenon resulting from the incompleteness of artistic creativity or perception. Changeability of aesthetic value "belongs to the very basis of aesthetic value, which is a process and not a state, *energeia* and not *ergon*."[16] The process of aesthetic evaluation is influenced by the development of the artistic structure itself, and by the developments in the structure of social life.

> The position of a work of art on a certain level of aesthetic value, the duration of its stay on that level, any change in position, or finally the complete removal from the scale of aesthetic value—all depend not only on the properties of the actual material work but on other factors as well. Only the work itself endures, passing from one time period into another, or from one place to another, one social milieu to another.[17]

Variation in aesthetic value exists at the same time and place as a result of the fact that "in a given society there is not just one level of poetic art, visual art, etc., but there are always several levels . . . and consequently several degrees of aesthetic value." The types of evaluation, then, not only live their own lives, they also meet and affect one another. A value that has lost its effectiveness in one level, for example, may enter another

14. Jan Mukarovsky, "Art as a Semiotic Fact," 83.
15. Jan Mukarovsky, *Aesthetic Function, Norm and Value as Social Facts*, 60–61.
16. Ibid., 64.
17. Ibid., 67.

level by sinking or rising. This multileveled nature of art "contributes to the complicated process of creating and transforming aesthetic values."[18]

The Individual in Aesthetic Evaluation

Mukarovsky recognized the place of the individual in aesthetic evaluation in the second stage of his development. Individual aesthetic judgment, however, was seen as reflecting "the collective nature and character of aesthetic evaluation." The power of this collective nature and control is evident in the fact that "for the evaluator, situated in a specific time and place, and in a given social milieu, any particular value of some work appears to him as necessary and constant. . . . The material ties entered into by the work as sign set in motion the attitude of a viewer toward reality. But the viewer is a social creature, a member of a collective." The attitude of the individual toward reality, then, is not the exclusive property of that individual. This is true even for the strongest personalities, and for weaker persons the attitude is almost totally determined by the social relationships in which the individual is involved.[19]

In the final stage Mukarovsky shifted attention from impersonal cultural codes to human beings as the subject and ultimate source of aesthetic interaction. The subject was viewed as an intersubjective agent interacting with the surrounding material world in various ways, depending upon the type of relationship and the dominance of either subject or the object. Four main functions are seen: practical, theoretical, symbolic, and aesthetic. The object dominates in the practical and symbolic functions. That is, the functional thrust is toward reality, directly through the mediation of sign. The subject dominates in the theoretical and aesthetic functions; in the theoretical, humanity is seeking to grasp the object cognitively and in the aesthetic, the act or process of evaluation is foregrounded. As Peter Steiner observes, "If the process of perception is the crucial aspect of the aesthetic interaction, then the subject's role in art must be redefined. He can no longer be seen as an irrelevant individual who merely superimposes his private

18. Ibid., 66
19. Ibid., 66, 67, 83.

associations upon a socially shared meaning, but as an active force indispensable to the genesis of meaning."[20]

The most systematic presentation of Mukarovsky's third stage was his lecture on "Intentionality and Unintentionality in Art" (1943). In this lecture, Mukarovsky discussed the special attitude necessary for the perception of artistic phenomena. The intentionality with which Mukarovsky is concerned is not the aim or purpose that is to be achieved by means of the work. It is the attitude of the perceiver. In works of art, according to Mukarovsky, it is such intentionality "which binds together the individual parts and components of a work into the unity that gives the work its meaning." During the perception of a work of art, the perceiver takes an attitude toward the object and immediately attempts to find in the organization of the work evidence of an arrangement that allows the work to be seen as a semantic whole. This unity is not to be found outside the work but in intentionality, "the force operating within the work which strives toward the resolution of the contradictions and tensions among its individual parts and components, thereby giving each of them a specific relation to the others and all of them together a unified meaning."[21]

Not all parts of a work can be unified in one simple uniform meaning, and what cannot be unified is considered as unintentional by the perceiver. This "unintentionality" is a concomitant phenomenon of intentionality and is very important for the aesthetic function. The boundary between the intentional and the unintentional is not static, for it is "the fate of every unintentionality that in time it will cross over into the artistic structure of the work, begin to be perceived as a component of it, and become intentionality."[22]

The problem of unintentionality and extra-aesthetic functions of the work of art are not the same, but they are related in that "an extra-aesthetic function can also . . . become a component of the unintentionality perceived in the work of art . . . if it appears to the perceiver as something ununifiable with the remaining semantic structure of the work."[23] In his 1946 lecture "On Structuralism,"

20. Steiner, "Jan Mukarovsky's Structural Aesthetics," xxxii–xxxiii.
21. Jan Mukarovsky, "Intentionality and Unintentionality in Art," 96.
22. Ibid., 115.
23. Ibid., 127.

Mukarovsky stressed that an emphasis on aesthetic function does not necessarily result in severing art from life. Not only are some works of art designed for particular kinds of social activities that are manifested in the structures of the works, but the functions of works of art may change over time. Mukarovsky even declares that a work is capable of fulfilling several functions at the same time and that the lack of unequivocal "content" makes the aesthetic function "transparent" and helpful for other functions.[24] In the case of the use of art in religion, for example, the religious factor is the dominant aspect as far as the church is concerned. Nevertheless, if the church admits art as an integral element of the cult, "it does so with the stipulation that the basic principles of art be subjected to outside directives, to norms which involve not only subject matter, but also artistic structure."[25]

When the creating or perceiving individual "adapts the structure of a work to a certain function, he does not exclude a priori any of the others. Otherwise he could not enter into live contact with reality through his work. If he forcibly simplified the functional richness of the work, he would also impoverish his own approach to reality and its stimulative capacity." When the functions of a work are looked at from the point of view of the individual, they appear "as a set of live energies which are in constant tension and conflict with one another"; they are seen not as separate compartments but as motion "which constantly changes the appearance of a work from perceiver to perceiver, from nation to nation, from period to period."[26]

"On Structuralism" also contains a concise description of the activity of the perceiver which emphasizes process.

> Every new partial sign which the perceiver apprehends during the process of perception (i.e., every component and every part of a work when entering the meaning-creating process of contexture) not only attaches itself to those which have penetrated previously into the perceiver's consciousness but also changes to a greater or lesser extent the meaning of everything that has preceded. And, conversely, everything that has preceded affects the meaning of every newly apprehended partial sign.[27]

24. Jan Mukarovsky, "On Structuralism," 11–12.
25. Mukarovsky, *Aesthetic Function*, 16.
26. Mukarovsky, "On Structuralism," 13.
27. Ibid., 8–9.

ROMAN INGARDEN: PHENOMENOLOGICAL THEORY

Ingarden, a Polish philosopher who studied under Edmund Husserl at Göttingen, published two major works in aesthetics that are important for reader-centered literary criticism: *The Literary Work of Art* (1931) and *The Cognition of the Literary Work of Art* (1937). The first volume deals with the question of the structuring of the literary work of art. What are the essential properties and conditions of that mode of being to which the literary work of art belongs? The second volume treats the processes leading to the cognition of the literary work of art. What are the possible ways of cognizing the literary work and what results can be expected from this cognition?

The Phenomenological Approach

Ingarden does not approach these questions as a literary critic concerned with literature on the level of actually existing works of literature but as a philosopher who is concerned with the formal structures common to all works of literature and with the nature of cognition which is a valid and true reconstruction of the literary work. The approach of Ingarden is essentially phenomenological not structural, however. David Michael Levin has evaluated the weakness of structuralism from the perspective of Ingarden's phenomenology:

> Structuralism . . . tends to be a one-sided approach; it concentrates, that is, on the formal structures of the literary work itself, while ignoring the distinctive structures and modalities of the aesthetic consciousness *for which* the work is an intentional object and *through which* the work is constituted as a unique aesthetic object. Structuralism, therefore, tends to miss—or at least, it cannot fully account for—such latent or dispositional properties of the work of art as come into being only through the constitutive intentionalities of an animating and reflective consciousness. Moreover, the one-sided object orientation which characterizes the method of structuralism means that structuralism cannot, as such, *show the ground* of the structures it has discerned in principles of the aesthetic consciousness. For . . . the possibility of grounding objective structures *presupposes* the possibility of demonstrating how these structures "accommodate" the aesthetic capacity of the human consciousness.[28]

28. David Michael Levin, "Foreword" to *The Literary Work of Art*, xxxi.

Levin suggests that Ingarden's phenomenological approach does not ignore the properties "contained" within the object structure of the literary work, but that his approach is able to account for those structures while also accounting for those properties "which acquire their ontological origin within the *subjective* conditions of our mode(s) of access." The work of art *itself*, then, is distinguished from the work as an aesthetic object that is constituted or concretized through the intentional acts of reading or performing it. Through the phenomenological approach, Ingarden is able to "construe the literary work of art as an ontological item that is at one and the same time an absolute aesthetic *unity* and also a logically differentiated *composite*."[29]

The Stratified Nature of the Work of Art

The literary work of art, in Ingarden's conceptualization, has two dimensions—linear and stratified. The most obvious is the linear dimension, the ordered sequence of sentences, groups of sentences, chapters, etc. As a consequence of this dimension, the work possesses a quasi-temporal extension from beginning to end, and certain properties of composition are to be seen, such as the characteristic of dynamic development.

The dimension given most attention by Ingarden is the layered dimension whereby a variety of strata exist simultaneously. Ingarden sees "the essential basic structure of the literary work" in its stratified structure and delineates four strata which differ from one another on the basis of material and the role each stratum plays in relation to the other strata and to the structure of the whole work. These four strata are:

> (1) the stratum of *word sounds* and the *phonetic formations* of higher order built on them; (2) the stratum of *meaning units* of various orders; (3) the stratum of manifold schematized *aspects* and aspect continua and series, and, finally (4) the stratum of *represented objectivities* and their vicissitudes.[30]

The strata of linguistic sound formations and meaning units. The phonetic stratum of linguistic sound formations is the essential constituent and the means of access to the literary work. The stratum of meaning units

---

29. Ibid., xxvii–xxviii.
30. Roman Ingarden, *Literary Work of Art,* 30.

(sentence meanings and the meanings of whole groups of sentences), nevertheless, is the stratum that "provides the structural framework for the whole work." This stratum, by its very essence, "requires all the other strata and determines them in such a way that they have their ontic basis in it and are dependent in their content on its qualities."[31]

Represented objects. The stratum of represented objects has to do with everything that is represented in the literary work of art, such as persons, things, events, states, and acts performed by persons.[32] This stratum seems to be the best known because the readers (as they follow the meaning intention of the text) focus attention first on the represented objects, persons, things, events, etc. The peculiarity of the represented objects may be overlooked by mistaking represented objects for real objects. The objects projected by units of meaning in literary works, however, are purely intentional objects that are "simulated in creative artistic imagination with the help of special acts of consciousness." The term "fictive" may be used instead of "purely intentional," but such objects, precisely as a result of the particular activity of the creative acts producing them, . . . attain the character of an independent reality. Once the creative intentionality has thus been actualized, it becomes to a certain degree binding for us."[33]

An essential property of represented objects that distinguishes them from real objects is their indeterminacy. Every real object is determined in every respect. It is true, of course, that when a perceiving subject apprehends real objects, the apprehension is incomplete. "However many determinations of a given object are apprehended up to a given moment, there are *always* other determinations still to be apprehended." Nevertheless, in itself the real object is not equivocal; it is universally determined. Real objects are also *absolutely individual*. They are not determined in a generalized way. For example, a real object is not just "colored" (with no particular color or shade), it has a particular shade of "red" or "yellow." The situation is different with represented objectivities. Spots of indeterminacy arise in represented objects that

31. Ibid., 29.
32. Ibid., 217–20.
33. Roman Ingarden, *The Cognition of the Literary Work of Art*, 40.

"in principle cannot be entirely removed by any finite enrichment of the content of a nominal expression."

> If, instead of simply "man" we say "an old, experienced man," we do remove, by the addition of these attributive expressions, certain spots of indeterminacy; but an infinite number still remains to be removed. They would disappear only in an infinite series of determinations. If, e.g., a story begins with the sentence: "An old man was sitting at a table," etc., it is clear that the represented "table" is indeed a "table" and not, for example, a "chair"; but whether it is made of wood or iron, is four-legged or three-legged, etc., is left quite unsaid and therefore—this being a purely intentional object—*not determined*. The material of its composition is altogether unqualified, although it must be some material. Thus, in the given object, its qualification is *totally absent;* there is an "empty" spot here, a "spot of indeterminacy."[34]

The represented object is not universally, unequivocally determined: "only a formal schema of infinitely many spots of determinacy is projected, but almost all remain unfilled."[35] The schematic structure of represented objects may be altered by the continual filling in of spots of indeterminacy, but the schematic structure cannot be removed.

Schematized aspects. The stratum of schematized aspects has to do with the appearance of represented objects, with the conditions under which such objects can become "intuitively given."[36] In the phenomenological conceptualization, every object (real or merely intentional) can become the object of an infinite number of mental acts distributed in time and among different individuals. The object in question, however, is transcendent with respect to the multiplicity of its possible correlative intentional acts. The transcendence of the object also means that it is never accessible in its absolute totality of properties.

It is easy to see this fact in respect to material objects. A book on the reader's desk is an object that can be variously differentiated from the background which envelops it (and which itself is constantly changing). As the reader moves around the desk, different aspects or properties of the book come into prominence. The fleeting images elude efforts at totalization. In the same way, it is the aspects of the portrayed object of

34. Ingarden, *Literary Work of Art,* 247–49.
35. Ibid., 250.
36. Ibid., 256.

a literary work of art that are experienced by the reader. The stratum of aspects is essential, therefore, for a literary work of art. It enables readers "to intuitively apprehend represented objects in predetermined types of modes of appearance" and thereby allows readers to "gain a certain power over represented objects by influencing their constitution." Aspects, however, possess their own properties and constitute their own aesthetic value qualities. Ingarden uses analogies from photography and sculpture to indicate that "the aspect stratum of a literary work contains its own aesthetic value qualities and can constitute its own aesthetic values according to the type of aspect and the nature of its content . . . " A gifted photographer selects from the many possible aspects of the given object one which will contain special aesthetically relevant features such as lighting, lines of perspective, or emotional shadings. A sculptor who is designing a monument of a human form to stand on a high pedestal will not simply adhere to purely anatomical proportions but will fashion the figure so that as it is seen from below it can evoke the intended "impression."[37]

Ingarden emphasized that "we have access to the world of portrayed objectivities always through the conceptual schemata; we never apprehend them directly in their intuitively accessible properties. We must first objectify these objects and 'clothe' them in an intuitive garb by the aid of aspects held in readiness."[38] It is true that aspects are impressed upon the reader by means of characteristics of the phonetic stratum and by the content of sentences, but in the work itself the aspects abide only in potential readiness and must be concretely experienced by the reader.

> The aspects are that which a perceiving subject experiences of a given object, and as such they demand a concrete perception or at least a vivid act of representation on the part of the subject if they are to be actually, concretely experienced. Only when they are concretely experienced do they exercise their proper function, that of bringing to appearance an object which has just been perceived.[39]

Metaphysical qualities. At least one literary scholar has observed a fifth stratum in Ingarden's conceptualization,[40] the stratum of metaphysical

37. Ibid., 276, 285.
38. Ingarden, *Cognition of Literary Work*, 230.
39. Ibid., 56.
40. René Wellek and Austin Warren, *Theory of Literature*, 152.

qualities; and, although Ingarden denies this as a necessary stratum in the being of a literary work of art, he does envision a "core" of the literary work beyond the four strata already discussed. From the perspective of this "core" everything else in the work is an accessory, everything else serves to bring this to the fore. This core is not an emotion or mood, instruction, ethical influence, the author's experience, or the author himself. The core consists of qualities that "reveal a 'deeper sense' of life and existence in general" and even "constitute this usually hidden 'sense.'" Ingarden cites such qualities as "the sublime, the tragic, the dreadful, the shocking, the inexplicable, the demonic, the holy, the sinful, the sorrowful, the indescribable brightness of good fortune, as well as the grotesque, the charming, the light, the peaceful, etc." He speaks of these "metaphysical qualities" as being "revealed" because they cannot be "grasped" as one grasps a mathematical theorem. They do not allow purely rational determination. "Instead they merely allow themselves to be, simply, one might almost say 'ecstatically,' *seen* in the determinate situations in which they are realized."[41]

> When we see them, the depths and primal sources of existence, to which we are usually blind and which we hardly sense in our daily lives, are "revealed" . . . to our mind's eye. But they not only reveal themselves to us; in looking at and in realizing them, we enter into primal existence. We do not merely *see* manifested in them that which is otherwise mysterious; instead, they *are* the primal [element] itself in one of its forms. But they can be fully shown to us only when they become reality. Thus the situations in which metaphysical qualities are realized and shown to us are the true high points of unfolding existence, and they are likewise the high points of the spiritual-psychic essences which we ourselves are. They are high points which throw a shadow on the rest of our lives; that is, they evoke radical transformations in the existence which is immersed in them, regardless of whether they bring with them deliverance or damnation.[42]

Concretization

The literary work of art and its concretization. In *The Literary Work of Art,* Ingarden distinguishes between the work of art itself and its concretizations that are constituted during the reading. The

41. Ingarden, *Literary Work of Art,* 291–92.
42. Ibid., 292.

complexity of a literary work and its total apprehension is such that "the experiencing ego has too much to do at once, as it were, and thus cannot give itself equally to all the components of this total apprehension." Only a few of the multiplicity of simultaneously experienced and interwoven acts are central. The rest are only "coeffected," coexperienced. "In the process, there is constant change with regard to which component acts (or experiences) are central at any given moment and which are developed only 'in passing,' only marginally." The fact that the same literary work is apprehended in various changing "aspects" is of decisive significance for the concretization of literary works. The manifold of aspects is generally different in two different readings, and therefore individual concretizations of the work must be distinguished from the work itself.[43]

Seven distinctions are specified by Ingarden: (1) In the literary work itself, word sounds appear as *typical Gestalt* qualities. In concretization, these qualities are carried by specific sounds and thereby obtain expression and concrete fullness. (2) In concretization, specific and unchanging word meanings and meaning contents are intermingled with meaning components that are not specific and therefore change from case to case. The concretization may determine objects more closely or even differently than they are predetermined by the work itself. (3) In a concretization, sentence meanings are taken over by the reader from words or sentences and are actually intended by the reader himself. (4) Aspects obtain concreteness and are raised to the level of imaginational experience. These concretely experienced aspects inevitably transcend the schematized content of aspects held in readiness in the work itself. (5) It is in the concretization of a literary work that "a truly explicit *appearance* of represented objectivities occurs." In the work itself "they are only indicated and held in a state of potentiality." (6) As a result of transformations in the strata of phonetic formations, units of meanings, and aspects, a number of spots of indeterminacy in represented objects are removed. "As a result, represented objects appear to us in concretizations in a much fuller form than they possess *de facto* in the work itself." (7) In concretizations the particular sequence of the parts of a literary work is transformed into a genuine sequence in

43. Ibid., 333–34.

phenomenal, concrete time. In the work itself the internal and external dynamics exist in a state of potentiality. The sequential order of the parts enables the dynamics of the work to achieve developed expression.[44]

Forms of interaction with the literary work of art. In *The Cognition of the Literary Work of Art,* Ingarden explicates most fully the processes entering into the cognition of the literary work of art. He distinguishes between cognition of "scientific" works and literary works and also between aesthetic concretization and other approaches to literary works. In the view of Ingarden the cognition of a scientific work "is nothing other than the correct understanding of its stratum of semantic units and, through that, the cognition of the 'reality' (in the proper sphere of being) which is transcendent to and intended in the work. Anything else which may occur during reading must be subordinated to this fundamental task."[45]

Even when a reader approaches a work as a literary work of art, however, interaction with the work may take different forms. A reader may approach a literary work merely for amusement without caring what it really is that gives enjoyment. Such a reader performs limited cognitive acts simply in order to find out how the story ends, but such cognition is done fleetingly, imprecisely, and idly. A reader seeking amusement is not concerned about faithful concretization of the work. A reader may approach the work itself in a diametrically opposite mode, with an "investigative" attitude. The reader then engages in a "preaesthetic cognition" of the work in order to discover the properties and elements in it that form the basis for the constitution of the aesthetic concretization. Although this type of cognition can begin only after the work has been read in the ordinary way, preaesthetic cognition is "more than a mere reading, insofar as special deliberations, comparisons, and analytic and synthetic reflections are carried out which do not appear in ordinary reading."[46] A reader may approach the *aesthetic concretization* of a work of art in an investigative attitude. The scientific apprehension depends upon the ability to share information about concretizations and

44. Ibid., 336–43.
45. Ingarden, *Cognition of Literary Work,* 164.
46. Ibid., 234.

to compare the concretizations and the values emerging in them. If aesthetic concretizations are formed with careful attention to the work embodied in them, the chance of a scientific study of the concretization is enhanced.

A reader may approach a work in an "aesthetic" attitude and go through processes involved in concretization. This is the process followed in normal reading practice. Various cognitive acts are involved: perceptual acts in which word signs or word sounds and phonetic formations of a higher order are apprehended, meaning-apprehending acts, and acts of imaginative beholding of represented objectivities and situations, and (if necessary) acts of imaginative beholding of the metaphysical qualities manifested in the objects and situations. Experiences of aesthetic enjoyment are aroused in the reader and various feelings and emotions are evoked by the reading in the mind of the reader.

Function and Cognition

In Ingarden's conceptualization, there is a necessary relationship between the method of cognition and the function of the work. Cognition of a work seen as a "scientific" work operates at a limited level. Cognition of even a literary work may also limit itself to the stratum of objectivities. For the practical man, for example, the stratum of objects exists for itself. The represented world is the real world that is conceived of as something existing only for itself and performing no function.

Although the conception of the literary work as expressing an "idea" is usually given a false interpretation in the opinion of Ingarden, it can be helpful for purposes of concretization if correctly interpreted. First of all, Ingarden denies that "idea" has to do with an assertion of "truth" about something that is present or should be present in the real world. The concept of "idea" is not basically the same as the concept of a true proposition. Next, Ingarden takes issue with the concept that the "idea" is "expressed" by the work of art. Such a concept "presupposes that the 'idea' does not belong to the work of art, is not contained in it, but rather is only supposed to be 'expressed' or somehow 'mediated' by it, as a structure foreign to the work, as some second object." Ingarden conceives of the "idea" of the literary work as "*in* the work itself or in that which is determined by it and belongs to it in an essential way." The idea is contained in the work in such a way that it is only when this factor has been made evident that the work has been apprehended completely.[47] The "idea" of the literary work of art is different for each work in that whatever content it has is determined "only on the basis of a particular analytical (although ultimately synthesizing) consideration of the individual work of art and of the aesthetic concretizations that are possible and appropriate to it." Nevertheless, a general statement can be made:

> The "idea" of the literary work of art is a "demonstrated," synthetic, essential complex of mutually modulated, aesthetically valent qualities which is brought to concrete appearance either in the work or by means of it. The aesthetically valent qualities lead to the intuitive constitution of a certain aesthetic value, and this value forms a whole, in intimate unity, with the basis on which it is founded (the literary work of art itself.)[48]

In the context of the question of the "adequacy" of the aesthetic experience of concretization, Ingarden develops the concept of the "idea" as the guide to the procedure of concretization, a procedure that "places certain demands on us as to the rules which must or should be followed, or the ways of concretizing which must or should be maintained in the further concretization, if a concretization in this form is finally to be constituted." The idea is the basis for judgment of adequacy, for the "aesthetic experience is 'adequate' when it leads to the constitution of a concretization which is the exact embodiment of the 'idea' indicated in it." In practical terms, it is important for a reader to apprehend the idea as early as possible and as clearly and distinctly as possible. The experience of concretization will then not be left to chance. Ingarden sees the necessity of some preliminary understanding of the work and some partial reconstruction of the work which serves as the basis for the constitution of an idea or a not-yet-actualized final form of concretization. Such an idea is implicit in the choice of a certain way of concretizing the work and becomes fixed as places of determinacy are filled out and potential elements of the work are actualized.[49]

The Life of a Literary Work

Although he is not primarily concerned with literary history, Ingarden affirms that a literary work "lives" in the sense that there are different

47. Ibid., 83.
48. Ibid., 85.
49. Ibid., 394.

phases in the course of its concretizations and also that the work itself (not merely its concretizations) undergoes various changes as a result of this process. The "life" of the literary work is related to traditions of understanding within which the work is concretized. In a given epoch, a reader is under the influence of a particular "literary atmosphere" that "introduces itself into the over-all cultural atmosphere of the time and maintains various functional relations with it." When the external circumstances are altered or when particularly strong individuals influence the literary tradition, the cultural atmosphere may change and concretizations will assume a visibly different form. The "manifold of concretizations" of a given literary work will not only be ordered temporally but will be relative to the atmosphere of a given era. The identity of the literary work is not lost. But the literary work itself does undergo change while maintaining its identity. Just as the literary work arises from subjective operations, it can be changed by analogous subjective operations such as the author's preparation of a second edition or a reader's establishment of different connections between sentences and introductions of new connections with conscious intent. In such cases the work itself "is changed in a conscious, intentional manner."[50]

FELIX VODICKA: LATER CZECH STRUCTURALISM

Literary History and Concretization

Felix Vodicka, a student of Mukarovsky, developed a theory of concretization that is related to the approach of his teacher and to that of Ingarden but is developed in the context of literary history. The traditional way the history of literature had dealt with the reception and concretization of an individual work was to assume a given value of the work and then to study how such a value was understood and discovered by criticism and readers. In this traditional approach, "differences and inconsistencies of evaluation were interpreted as errors and the lack of literary taste on the basis of the assumption that there exists one single aesthetic 'norm.'" Vodicka, however, declares that the failure of literary historians, students of aesthetics, and critics to agree on such a "correct"

---

50. Ingarden, *Literary Work of Art*, 349–53.

norm is an indication that such a norm and single evaluation based on such a norm do not exist. The truth is that "a work can be the object of a multiple evaluation whereby the form of the work changes unceasingly in the consciousness of the perceiver (his concretization)."[51]

Placing the study of concretization in the broad context of literary history and development seems to Vodicka to be a way of avoiding an extreme subjectivism. The literary historian is able to study the literary work as an aesthetic object, to trace the incorporation of the work in the system of actual literary values, and, thereby, to uncover a context for observing the work which is not time bound and subjective.

Interdependence of Factors in Concretization

Vodicka's theory of concretization is influenced by his literary-historical task; and although the term "concretization" is adopted from the work of Ingarden, a somewhat different emphasis is placed on the conceptualization. Concretization is not only a matter of filling in places of indeterminacy in the higher strata so as to gain a concrete form of a specific work. Concretization has to do with all strata and with the total structure perceived in changing contexts. The "author," literary categories such as genre, literary organizations, literary epochs, the literature of an entire nation, and literature as a whole are objects of aesthetic evaluation that must be "concretized" just as the work itself. The "author" as a literary fact, for example (not as a historical character), underlies different evaluations. But the "author" is related to the total context in a dynamic fashion in that the totality of the temporally constrained literary norms influences the reader-critic in the concretization of the author. Vodicka acknowledges that "we can objectively establish individual components of the author-structure and in this perspective they have for some time been the object of scientific research," but what he considers important is the fact that the author-structure is to be understood (just as the structure of a single work) not as the sum of its components but as "a dynamically organized system with a dominating tendency." This structure-organization (of the author as of the work) is not firmly established before interaction with the literary work; it comes into existence

---

51. Felix Vodicka, "Die Literaturgeschichte, Ihre Probleme und Aufgaben," 69–70.

through concretization.[52] The same is true for higher structural units, for literary units such as genre, and for literature as seen from different perspectives. These units, just as elements of the author-structure, are not only the objects of scientific research, they are aesthetically evaluated on the basis of contemporary norms.

The Structuring of a Work of Art

The factors Vodicka sees as playing a part in the field of literature (and in the concretization of an individual literary work) are seen in part because of his concern with literary history. His view of the structure of the individual work may also be influenced by this interest. In his early work, Vodicka follows a structuralist conceptualization of the literary work of art as a system formed out of elements bound to each other in different ways, but he did not give attention to the description of the literary work in detail. In his 1948 book on the beginning of the neo-Czech belles-lettres (*The Beginnings of Modern Czech Prose Fiction: A Contribution to the Literary History of Jungmann's Era*), he did give a theoretical statement as to the structural characteristic of the thematic construction of an epic work.[53] From the perspective of theme, a work is formed by means of motifs that are bound together into larger units or planes which extend throughout a work. Action is one of the planes. On the plane of action, motifs are joined in a temporal and causal sequence. Major characters also form a plane; these characters are necessary to carry out the action. But the actions and characters are united with local, temporal, and other motifs which form a third plane, that of environment. This environment is not merely material; it is also the total social, psychological, and imaginary atmosphere in which the characters live and carry out actions.

Vodicka's analysis of the different planes of a work is related to the reader-oriented approach to literature because of the fact that individual motifs are not joined in a static way with particular planes. The planes (or contexts of action, character, and environment) are in competition with each other for the attention of the reader. This means that a single motif is not always united by the reader in a given plane but can be

---

52. Felix Vodicka, "Die Konkretisation des Literarischen Werks," 114.
53. Sections of this book are contained in *Die Struktur der Literarischen Entwicklung*.

incorporated into different planes or contexts with different meanings. The relationship becomes even more dynamic when it is seen that although each plane of motifs has a characteristic means of expression (actions being expressed in narrative, characters in characterizations, and environment in description) the means of expression may be altered. Action may be described instead of narrated, for example, and character and environment may be expressed through narrative.[54]

The observation of the structure of a literary work against the background of the structure of the actual literary tradition under changing temporal, local, and social circumstances means that the structure of the total work in concretization is given a new character again and again. But in the specific concretizations by individual readers, it is not just the actual literary tradition that is at work. The external environment of reception, the psychological disposition of the reader, and other subjective factors enter into the reading.[55] Moreover, it must be remembered that within groups of readers "several levels exist beside each other which are oriented to different norms." There are different levels because of the co-existence of different generations (the coexisting sons, fathers, and grandfathers may have different literary norms) and the vertical stratification of the literary public (literarily and aesthetically cultured readers, the broad reading community, and readers of peripheral products). There are also differences because of different geographical locations.[56]

Of importance for reader-oriented interpretation at the critical level is Vodicka's treatment of the relationship between concretizations and the critical description of concretizations. The descriptions of concretizations vary. Academic descriptions are different from impressionistic and ideological descriptions. Description, however, is related to concretization, for the critical description will support the particular concretization or evaluation of a work in its argumentation. One context for critical description may emphasize the psychological development of the author. Another context may emphasize the question of artistic design. The different contexts, then, influence the perception of the reader-critic and her or his concretization and evaluation of the literary work.[57]

54. Felix Vodicka, "Jungmanns Übersetzung von Chateaubriands Atala," 298–99.
55. Vodicka, "Konkretisation," 105–6.
56. Vodicka, "Literaturgeschichte," 63–64.
57. Vodicka, "Konkretisation," 106–11.

JURIJ LOTMAN: SOVIET SEMIOTICS

Lotman is a contemporary Soviet semiotician who continues the formalist-structuralist tradition and who has a conceptualization of the structure of the artistic text that accommodates apparently opposing views of the function of the text. Lotman's work is marked by development, recapitulating in a formal way earlier developments in formalism and structuralism. He has moved from theorizing about the relationship of elements within a work, to the relationship of literature to the other arts in a given culture, to a semiotic approach to culture as "text." For our purposes, we will highlight his theories of the structure of a literary text, how a reader discovers and creates meaning, and the meanings that are associated with the text.

The Structure and Function
of Literary Texts

Lotman sees texts as fulfilling two basic functions: the transmission of meanings and the generation of new meanings. The transmission of meaning is best accomplished by a text in a code such as an artificial language that is shared fully by speaker and hearer. The text may be seen as "a passive container, a mere receptacle for content inserted into it from outside." The generation of new meaning is the function of artistic texts that stand at the opposite pole to the artificial text. The literary text, for Lotman, is not a text that is purged of meaning (as with the formalists) but one that is overloaded with meanings due to a "total coding through a double code." The first encoding is in the system of the language of the author, a natural language such as English, French, or German. Artistic and nonartistic texts share in this encoding. The vital characteristic of artistic texts (or of nonartistic texts that also have artistic functions), however, is that of encoding in a "language" that is not simply a natural language but is a "secondary system" superimposed on natural language.[58]

> In applying to the work of literature a whole hierarchy of supplementary codes (those of epoch, of genre, or of style), which function within an entire national body or a narrowly delimited group (right down to individuals), we are faced in one and the same text with the most varied sets of significant

58. Jurij Lotman, "The Future for Structural Poetics," 503.

elements and, consequently, a complicated hierarchy of strata of meanings additional to those of the non-literary text.[59]

The reduction of the artistic text to the transmission of specific constant information misconceives the function of the artistic text. Lotman does not deny the possibility of the analysis of texts with the use of static models resulting from independent codes, but he does deny the explanation of the structures and functions of the text as the structure and function of any one of the static models or of the simple accumulation of models. He emphasizes that "no static model reflects the structure of a text, but only the structure of one of the constructive principles on the crossing of which the text lives."[60]

Lotman uses the analogy of the chemical analysis of sea water to distinguish different conceptualizations of the structure of the artistic text. The conceptualization of the text as conveying specific constant information is comparable to the reasoning of the chemist who sees in sea water a particular case of water in general. When the chemist separates off the formula H_2O, he has completed the analysis and refuses to investigate the residue of its composition as being "outside the system." The view of the text as an addition of static codes corresponds to a second stage when the researcher discovers the presence of many other ingredients in sea water. By setting out the different chemical formulas of the other ingredients, he acknowledges the mixture of different substances to be a fact. The view of the text that Lotman advocates, however, is comparable to a third stage when sea water acquires for the researcher "the character of an integral chemical mechanism with its own structure and internal self-regulation combining a unity of dynamic and static principles, a mechanism manifesting qualities and potentialities which would not be characteristic of any of its separate components or parts."[61]

The description of one structural level of a text limits "the rich semantics of a text" and is to be regarded as "a purely heuristic stage in the study of a text." Description of individual structural levels "are not intended to reduce the artistic text to unambiguous systems and then

---

59. Jurij Lotman, "The Content and Structure of the Concept of 'Literature,' " 341.
60. Jurij Lotman, "On Some Principle Difficulties in the Structural Description of a Text," 58.
61. Lotman, "Future for Structural Poetics," 504.

provide the ultimate interpretation of a work of art." Nevertheless, Lotman maintains a structural perspective. The things that are original and unique in a work of art are not accessible only to impressionistic "empathy." They are involved in structure and precise analyses, but "they occur at the intersection of many structures and belong to them simultaneously, 'playing' with the many meanings that arise in the process."[62]

The Role of the Reader

The question of the role of the reader in the process of reading is discussed by Lotman in terms of his conceptualization of opposition, system, and the multiple coding of a literary work of art. Some important oppositions seen by Lotman are: artistic text versus nonartistic text; aesthetics of identity versus aesthetics of opposition; "author's" perspective versus "reader's" perspective; sensuous pleasure versus intellectual pleasure; and the text as viewed by a researcher versus the text as viewed by a reader. All of these are related to the process of reading and interpretation.

Artistic and nonartistic texts. A nonartistic text has the function of transmitting meanings, and artistic texts have the function of the generation of new meanings. A basic condition for aesthetic communication, then, is determination of the nature of the text. This is not so simple a matter because the boundary between artistic and nonartistic texts has been and is drawn differently in different cultures and by different readers. A text that is nonartistic for the writer may be perceived aesthetically by a reader, and an artistic text may be perceived by a reader as nonartistic information because "the reader is not capable of identifying it with any of those forms of organization which satisfy his definition of art."[63] The problem is compounded by the fact that multiple functions are served by the same text. The work of art itself may be approached for nonaesthetic purposes. It "can be used as material for the observation of historical, socio-economic or philosophical problems; it can serve as source for witness of the norms for everyday life or of legal

---

62. Lotman, *The Structure of the Artistic Text*, 300.
63. Ibid., 287.

and ethical norms." There is a dialectical relationship between the artistic and the nonartistic functions of the text that is not simply due to the fact that in real life the same text carries out several functions. Lotman declares that "in order to carry out a definite artistic task a text must at the same time have an ethical, political, philosophical, promotional function. And vice versa, if a text is to fulfill a definite function, such as a political function, it must also realize an aesthetic function."[64]

Aesthetics of identity and opposition. The aesthetics of identity versus the aesthetics of opposition has to do with different ways of perceiving the artistic work. A common code may be used, one agreed upon by the author and reader (aesthetics of identity); or the reader may impose a code different from that used by the author or even create a new code (aesthetics of opposition). Lotman says certain artistic systems, such as folklore and medieval art, "judge a work according to its observation of certain rules rather than their violation." The author and the audience unconditionally assume the common nature of the aesthetic language and through certain devices, such as the situation of performance or other extratextual conditions, the reader is given the cue to the "only possible artistic language of the given text." The meanings discerned by the reader, however, may differ, the reader perceiving a new message. In the aesthetics of opposition, the author follows his own, original methods and rules in opposition to those that are familiar to the reader.[65]

Perspectives of the author and the reader. The distinction between the perspective of the author and the perspective of the reader in the process of communication is seen by Lotman as helpful in envisioning the process of communication. The author moves in the direction of complication and analysis, the reader in the direction of simplicity and synthesis. By author and reader, Lotman is not simply speaking of real authors and real readers. "In each real author and real reader, both 'author' and 'reader' exist in varying proportions. . . ." The author is

---

64. Jurij Lotman, *Analysis of the Poetic Text,* 7.
65. Lotman, *Structure of Artistic Text,* 289, 24.

seen by Lotman as creating a text "that functions simultaneously within several code systems. Each new part must awaken an awareness of already existing codes and be projected onto them; this correlation lends it new meanings and gives new meanings to parts of the text that previously seemed comprehensible." The reader, on the other hand, is inclined to "view an artistic text as a normal speech message, extracting information from each episode and reducing the composition to a temporal sequence of separate events."[66]

Sensual and intellectual pleasure. The distinction between author and reader is related to the distinction between sensuous pleasure of sense perception and intellectual pleasure of information reception in the process of reading. Sense perception is the process of subjecting the material of the text to a variety of codes in an attempt to reduce the material to a system or a structural relation. The analogy of the process of digestion of food is used to illustrate the process of sense perception:

> Let us take as a text . . . a piece of food we are eating. The whole process of digestion can be divided into stages of interaction between nerve receptors, acids and enzymes. On every level some portion of what was not assimilated on the previous level, that is, which did not carry information, which was extra-systemic and neutral, joins in the active process of metabolism, becomes systemic and yields the information contained within itself.[67]

An emphasis on sensuous pleasure "entails the multiple application of diverse codes" and "strives for protraction." Intellectual pleasure is the result of the reduction of the variegated materials to one system. It comes about by the "application of a code or a small number of logically connected codes to the message." Intellectual pleasure is instantaneous, "an expression, like a nutshell, is cracked open only to be thrown away."[68]

Reader and researcher. The reader and the researcher view the text differently, according to Lotman. The reader is attempting to decode a particular text and views everything superimposed on the text as a

66. Ibid., 295.
67. Ibid., 58.
68. Ibid., 58–59.

hierarchy of codes that reveal the hidden semantics of that one particular work of art. The reader, then, is interested in how a work is structured from the perspective of its "functional unity." The researcher sees a hierarchy of texts moving from subtexts of the author's text (such as the phonological level and the grammatical level) to the broadest concept of text—the literature of the twentieth century, for example. For the researcher, "the hierarchy of the texts is real, almost as if one text were inserted into the other." The researcher is interested in the mechanics of the code on the various levels and the interaction of the codes, and he is interested in the fullest possible description of all levels. He is even interested in how the *study* of the work is structured. Lotman shares the interest of the specialist and the reader, but he acknowledges the unrealistic nature of a description of even a small text. The sheer volume of description of all connections which arise in the text as well as all extratextual relations which could be ascertained make a complete description impossible.[69]

Processing a Text

The activity of the actual reader involves the two procedures of analysis and synthesis that are implicit in all the oppositions discussed above. Analysis, the breaking up of the text into its component parts, is more compatible with the aesthetics of opposition, the author's perspective, and sensuous pleasure. Analysis, however, cannot exist without synthesis which is more compatible with the aesthetics of identity, the reader's perspective, and intellectual pleasure. The analytical task of the reader, then, must be related to the synthetic task. It is only as the reader is able to create a system out of the elements of the text that "information" is obtained.

Lotman sees a period of preparation prior to the actual process of analysis and synthesis. First is the acknowledgment that the text is being approached as artistic speech rather than as ordinary speech. What would be redundant when the text is seen as ordinary speech becomes semantically distinctive when the reader sees the text as artistic. Such an artistic perspective allows the reader to comprehend the complex fabric of recurrences, comparisons, and oppositions in the text.[70]

69. Ibid., 280, 55.
70. Ibid., 294.

The actual processing by the reader involves the correlation of the textual elements with various codes. The natural language, of course, is basic for the construction and analysis of the artistic text's secondary codes. The initial process of analysis of reading involves the breaking up of the text into its temporal (syntagmatic) segments. For a poetic text, this involves the phoneme, morpheme, line, strophe, and chapter. In prose, the word, sentence, paragraph, and chapter are involved. The text will then be analyzed on the basis of different semantic levels, such as that of character types. This analysis is possible because of the code of the natural language, but other codes are involved—codes and groups of codes that the reader has in her or his consciousness. These codes have to do with categories such as poetry/prose, genre, plot types, and literary schools.[71]

Lotman suggests that a reader comes to a choice of a decoding system on the basis of an initial reception of elements of texts. No matter the initial choice of decoding systems, the reader immediately begins to receive signs that cannot be coded in the chosen system. These may include repetitions or equivalences in the text, contingencies, and grammatical and syntactic constructions. On all levels of the planes of expression and content these signs appear. The careful reader will see all these as bearers of meaning that cannot be pushed aside. So the reader constructs a second system that allows the decoding of the signs. From that point, the new system is superimposed on the first.[72]

This procedure on the part of the reader is a necessary result of the law of "the concurrence of structurally heterogeneous segments," one of the basic structural principles of an artistic text. The juxtaposing of units that are incompatible in one system forces a reader to construct an additional system on a higher level where the incompatibility is eliminated.[73]

The semantic effect of an abrupt change of style is illustrated by some lines from Pushkin:

> *When she stands before me,*
> *Slender and bright eyed* . . .
> I think, "She was divorced
> On the feast of Elijah!"

71. Ibid., 92.
72. Ibid., 73.
73. Ibid., 280.

In the first two lines, the reader is referred to a type of lyric style. The second two lines are in marked contrast. "A complex collision is effected between the code system of the lyrics of popularized Romanticism in the 1820's and ironical poetry on themes of everyday life." The codes are perceived sequentially by the reader, but what occurs is the "mutual superimposition" of the codes and interpretations. Each of these codes is taken, not by itself, but "in relation to the other . . . within the semantic relations of mutual recoding."[74]

Lotman emphasizes that in artistic systems, the structure is never fully automated; the heterogeneity is never fully canceled out. Some type of ordering of texts or groups of texts is always in conflict with material that is nonordered in relation to it. To some extent, this is the result of the fact that extratextual systems are involved in a work of art and that "traits of individual subjective development and objective historical development" cause a constant process of change in the reader's consciousness. This means that the "degree of structural activeness of certain elements in the intricate complex of the artistic whole is constantly changing for the reader." As a reader integrates elements of one level into the system by means of a code, then structural dominance is transferred to another level that has not become automatized as far as the reader is concerned. The consciousness of this process of change may play a part in the reader's interaction with the text. The reader will constantly realize that "there may be other meanings besides those perceived at the moment." Each interpretation may not only preserve the memory of previous meanings, but it will recognize "the possibility of future meanings."[75]

Meaning and Interpretation

Lotman's conceptualization does not result in the dissolution of meaning and interpretation nor in the "static simultaneous coexistence of different meanings." It results in an "abundance of meanings and possible interpretations in the text." But there is meaning, and there is validity in interpretation that Lotman sees as "the recoding of specifically artistic information into the language of a non-artistic modeling system." Such a recoding is of necessity the reduction of the

74. Ibid., 74.
75. Ibid., 135, 300, 67.

artistic text. "Artistic and non-artistic models have a different number of dimensions," therefore "the recoding of artistic texts with two or more planes into any monoplaner non-artistic language will not give us a one-to-one correspondence." Nevertheless, the "very role that art plays in society" involves an "endeavor to correlate artistic models with ethical, philosophical, political, and religious models." The recoding of the meaning of an artistic model into the language of the nonartistic modeling system is the only way to achieve the "strictly monosemous definition" that is required.[76]

Lotman's view of the structure of the artistic text and his model of reading are comprehensive and dynamic, including natural language and conventional meaning, and meanings that remain potential but which nevertheless influence the meanings assigned at a given historical moment. The conceptualization is not one of anarchy but one of dynamic order and reordering.

> New structures which enter into a text or the extra-textual background of a work of art do not cancel out the old meanings, but enter into semantic relations with them. A structure that enriches the informational content of a text differs from a destructive heterogeneous structure in that everything heterogeneous which can be correlated in some way with the structure of the authorial text ceases to be noise.[77]

The key to meaning is the reader. The text is able "to correlate with the reader and provide him with just the information he needs and is prepared to receive . . . ."[78] One of the reasons art is able to render its indispensable service to humankind, and one of the ways, indeed, is that

> it transmits different information to different readers in proportion to each one's comprehension; it provides the reader with a language in which each successive portion of information may be assimilated with repeated reading. It behaves as a kind of living organism which has a feedback channel to the reader and thereby instructs him.[79]

---

76. Ibid., 67–68.
77. Ibid., 75.
78. Ibid., 24.
79. Ibid., 23.

CHAPTER *3*

European Contributions

Basic theoretical foundations for reader-oriented literary criticism were set in place by the formalist-structuralist tradition. In that tradition, the literary work is viewed as a structural system. But the system is dynamic because of its incomplete nature that invites the involvement of the reader and because of the relationship of the text and the reader to dynamic extratextual systems and structures.

The objective nature of the literary work, the control over the reader exercised by the work, and the necessity of validating the interpretative work of the reader have been emphasized in some of the theoretical discussions. Others have emphasized the freedom of the reader in actualizing not only the literary work but also all the other systems with which the work is related and that bear upon its meaning and interpretation. In the European literary context in which the formalist-structuralist influences have been felt, the same oppositions have been at work. This chapter will examine developments in the study of narrative in French structuralism; attempts among European scholars to develop models for text processing; and the work of Hans Robert Jauss and Wolfgang Iser on the history of reception and effect (impact).

NARRATOLOGY

The formalist-structuralist tradition became influential in France as it was mediated through Roman Jakobson, who was in exile with Claude Lévi-Strauss in the United States during the Second World War. In

France, the structuralist movement may be seen as standing in opposition to the positivism or factuality favored in the literary studies represented by Gustav Lanson as well as to the individuality stressed in existentialism.

Vladimir Propp: Syntagmatic Analysis

Although Lévi-Strauss must be considered the father of French structuralism, it was the 1928 Russian work of Vladimir Propp (translated into English in 1958, French in 1970, and German in 1972) that stimulated the development of structural narratology in the 1960s. Narratology (including the work of Lévi-Strauss) can best be understood against the background of Propp's contribution. Propp analyzed a corpus of one hundred Russian fairy tales from a "morphological" perspective, that is, with the purpose of describing the tale according to its component parts and to show the relationship between these components. Prior to the work of Propp, the "motif" was considered to be the basic unit of the folk tale, and countless motifs were discerned. Propp, however, emphasized not motifs but "functions," actions at the formal or abstract level, limited in number. Propp illustrated the function of folk tales by means of the following examples:

1. A tsar gives an eagle to a hero. The eagle carries the hero away to another kingdom.

2. An old man gives Sucenko a horse. The horse carries Sucenko away to another kingdom.

3. A sorcerer gives Ivan a little boat. The boat takes Ivan to another kingdom.

4. A princess gives Ivan a ring. Young men appearing from out of the ring carry Ivan to another kingdom, and so forth.[1]

---

1. Vladimir Propp, *Morphology of the Folktale*, 19–20. The work of Propp illustrates the attempt to quantify the sorts of data found in narrative. His work has been influential in the study of different types of narrative. Alan R. Dundes used the work of Propp to study North American folk tales. Instead of the term "function," Dundes used the term "motifeme" (borrowed from Kenneth Pike) for the minimum unit. On the basis of his research, Dundes concludes that "there are definite recurrent sequences of motifemes and these sequences constitute a limited number of distinct patterns which empirical observation reveals are the structural bases of North American folk tales" (*The Morphology of North American Indian Folktales*, 61). Erhardt Güttgemanns has used the work of Propp, Dundes, and others to study New Testament narrative. Through a restructuring of the motifemes according to logical laws of relationships (contradiction, contrariness, implication, and complementa-

There are different characters, but the characters perform the same *sorts* of actions or functions. Propp concluded that in the folk tales a multiplicity of characters are to be seen in contrast with the small number of functions (or the acts of characters defined from the perspective of their significance for the course of the entire action). The result of Propp's analysis of the Russian folk tales is the following: only thirty-one different functions can be identified. Moreover, the sequence in which the functions appear is constant; not every folk tale contains all thirty-one functions, but the absence of some functions does not alter the sequence of those present. Propp defines a tale morphologically as the development that proceeds from "villainy" or "lack" (something that disturbs an initial situation of equilibrium) through intermediate functions to "marriage" or some other function that serves as a denouement. In an actual tale, of course, there may be several "tales" or sequences from "villainy" to "marriage"—each new act of villainy or new lack creates a new move or sequence.

Propp also reduced the multiplicity of different characters that carry out functions in the tale to a limited number of character-types or spheres of action: the villain, the donor, the helper, the princess and her father (a sought-for person), the dispatcher, the hero, and the false hero. A relationship is established between the thirty-one functions and the seven character-types in that the same functions are always carried out by the same character-type.

For Propp, the key to analysis was the sequence of moves or functions. The structural method of Propp has, therefore, been termed "syntagmatic." The structure or formal organization is described following the chronological order or linear sequence of elements in the tale.

Claude Lévi-Strauss: Paradigmatic Analysis

The "paradigmatic" structural analysis of Lévi-Strauss differs from the sequential analysis in that it is not the chronologically ordered sequences that are bearers of the real meaning. It is the schemata that are

---

tion), he obtains a "narrative lexicon" consisting of sixteen binary pairs. For him, these sixteen pairs are the beginning point of any structural analysis. ("Narrative Analyse synoptischer Texte," 51.)

of most interest. The schemata exist simultaneously, superimposed on one another on planes with different levels of abstraction. The organization of sequences and schemata is compared by Lévi-Strauss to a melody composed for several voices. The melody is held in bond by the horizontal melodic lines and by the vertical contrapuntal schemata (settings).

To read a myth only line after line, from left to right, does not result in an apprehension of the myth as a totality because the basic meaning of the myth is not conveyed by the sequence of events. The meaning is conveyed by "bundles of events" which appear at different moments in the story. Lévi-Strauss says that

> we have to read the myth more or less as we would read an orchestral score, not stave after stave, but understanding that we should apprehend the whole page and understand that something which was written on the first stave at the top of the page acquires meaning only if one considers that it is part and parcel of what is written below on the second stave, the third stave and so on.[2]

Lévi-Strauss illustrates this with the theme of the renunciation of love in Wagner's tetralogy, *The Ring*. The theme is introduced in the *Rhinegold* when the Rhine maiden tells Alberich that he can conquer the gold only by renouncing all human love. In the *Valkyrie*, the theme reappears at the moment Siegmund discovers that Sieglinde is his sister and falls in love with her. The two will initiate an incestuous relationship, thanks to the sword that Siegmund will tear away from the tree. In the last act of the *Valkyrie*, Wotan, the king of the gods, surrounds his daughter, Brunhilde, with fire and condemns her to a long magical sleep. It could be thought that Wotan is renouncing love because he is renouncing his love for his daughter. Lévi-Strauss suggests that an understanding of the mysterious reappearance of the theme of the renunciation of love is gained only by putting the three events together, treating the three as one and the same event. On the three different occasions there is a treasure to be pulled away—gold in the depths of the Rhine, a sword in the tree (the symbolic tree of life or of the universe), the woman, Brunhilde, out of the fire. It is the recurrence of the theme which suggests that the gold, the sword, and Brunhilde are the same:

2. Claude Lévi-Strauss, *Myth and Meaning*, 45.

the gold as a means to conquer power; the sword as a means to conquer love.

> The fact that we have a kind of coalescence between the gold, the sword, and the woman is . . . the best explanation we have of the reason why, at the end of the *Twilight of the Gods*, it is through Brunhilde that the gold will return to the Rhine; they have been one and the same, but looked at through different angles.[3]

In his analysis of myths, Lévi-Strauss also finds and uses what he considers to be an innate tendency of the human mind to work by a process of binary analysis. This binary opposition (nature versus culture, raw versus cooked, etc.) is not merely grounded in the order of things but represents an antinomy of the human mind. The oppositions are transformed in myths by inversion and in metaphor and other figures. Along with the opposition there is a tendency of the human mind toward mediation of the opposition.

A. J. Greimas: Accommodation of Different Approaches

In the work of French narratologists, both the syntagmatic approach of Propp and the paradigmatic approach of Lévi-Strauss have been influential. Greimas has accommodated the two approaches by distinguishing between different levels.[4] The discursive level is the level of the narrative with a succession of events and with characters who act and are acted upon. Here the anthropomorphic perspective is dominant and the linear approach of Propp is appropriate. The same narrative, however, may be seen as existing on a structural level where static, logical, nonlinear elements and relationships are operative. Here, the paradigmatic analysis of Lévi-Strauss is appropriate. Although the different levels may be seen as "isotopes" of the same narrative with an interplay of elements of the different levels, it is more common to see the "surface" discursive level as a result of "deeper," "non-temporal" logical relations.

The most profound level is the level of logical relationships or the "elementary structure of signification." The terms in this structure are

3. Ibid., 48.
4. A. J. Greimas and F. Rastier, "The Interaction of Semiotic Constraints."

defined in relationship to each other. In the conceptualization of Greimas, binary oppositions are not the only relationships emphasized. The contradictory and contrary relationships that can be established logically from any starting point are stressed. For example, the opposition rich/poor would be expanded by Greimas to include "not rich" and "not poor." "Poor" is in a contrary relationship to "rich," but "not rich" and "not poor" are in a contradictory relationship to "rich" and "poor." In the same way "black" and "white" are contrary terms to which "non-black" and "non-white" stand in a relationship of contradiction. "Rich," on the other hand, *implies* "not-poor" and "poor" *implies* "not-rich," so relationships of implication are also involved.

Greimas views the four terms of the logical elementary structure of signification not simply as expressing timeless logical relationships and relationships of implication but also as indicating succession, the route that a narrative will take in the movement from poverty to wealth, for example. From the binary opposition of Lévi-Strauss, movement can be made to the discursive level by the progressive expansion of the logical relationships and by the investment of the abstract "grammar" by anthropomorphic representation. The functions and character-types of Propp can be integrated with the logical paradigmatic approach of Lévi-Strauss.

Other narratologists in the quest for laws of a universal narrative grammar agree with Greimas on the basic principles: the distinction between different planes of narrative structure, the possibility of articulating the series of events in sequences of action, and the development of a "lexicon" of narrative and rules of combination of such narrative units. Nevertheless, there is disagreement on the relationship of the logical base to the narrative itself and on the most appropriate way to model the rules and invariant patterns followed in narrative formation.

Claude Bremond

Bremond's disagreement with Greimas has to do with the dynamics of the narrative or the freedom of the narrator. Bremond charges that Greimas's model is static and nontemporal, emphasizing the interplay of logical relationships that transcend and ignore the "becoming" of the narrated events. Bremond's emphasis is on the "becoming," the dynamics of the narrative. Bremond's model sees the narrative developing as a result of decisions made at strategic points in the story, decisions as to which direction the story should take. The decisions are essentially choices from among possibilities that could continue and complete the narrative. Beginning with some desired objective (potentiality), there is either the development of a procedure to reach the objective (actualization) or an inertia that hinders the actualization. When the choice is actualization and a procedure is developed, the objective may be reached (success) or missed (failure). The basis pattern can be diagrammed simply:[5]

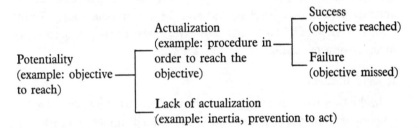

Potentiality
(example: objective
to reach)

Actualization
(example: procedure in
order to reach the
objective)

Success
(objective reached)

Failure
(objective missed)

Lack of actualization
(example: inertia, prevention to act)

Tzvetan Todorov

In Todorov's early work, a narrative was conceived of as the syntagmatic projection of paradigmatic relations. In his treatment of the logic of actions in "Les catégories du récit littéraire" (1966), for example, Todorov combined Bremond's triadic syntagmatic model with the logical four-term model. In his *Grammaire du Décaméron* (1969) Todorov analyzes more carefully the syntactical level, viewing a narrative as analogous to a sentence. *Proper nouns* are agents (subjects or objects of the action), *verbs* are actions that modify the situation, *adjectives* relate to the quality of the agents. The actions can be categorized as to *status* (negation is one possible status), *modality* (imperative and optative for example), and *point of view*.

The minimal narrative is a sequence that is perceived by the reader as a finished story because of the modified repetition of the initial clause. That is, there is a shift from one equilibrium to another. The two

---

5. Claude Bremond, "Morphology of the French Folktale," 249.

moments of equilibrium (a stable but not static relationship) are separated by a time of imbalance involving degradation and improvement.

Todorov is interested in the general and abstract. He seeks "a theory of the structure and operation of the literary discourse" so the "existing works of literature appear as particular instances that have been realized."[6] Nevertheless, he does have an interest in the particular instances, and he gives specific suggestions on how to move from the abstract level to that of the individual tale. The organization of the story may be studied at a concrete rather than an abstract level. The concrete actions that incorporate the abstract pattern may be studied thematically. In rhetorical study, the type of discourse that is used to embody the abstract pattern may be examined and the action seen from different points of view. The particular narrative, however, is still seen as an instance of a realization of an abstract type.

Roland Barthes

In the later work of Barthes, the work of the structuralists is used to emphasize not the abstract structure which underlies particular narratives but the individual and concrete. The task of seeing "all the world's stories . . . within a single structure" is not only an exhausting task; "it is also an ultimately undesirable task," in the opinion of Barthes, "for the text thereby loses its difference." The approach of Barthes emphasizes the reader and the possibilities the text offers readers to arrive at satisfying plural meaning. The structure of the text is such that it involves the reader in a process of analysis without a *final* synthesis or end. The text is like a group of threads braided together to form a core. The material for the textual braid is a group of codes, existing in a linear and in a nonlinear relationship. The code of actions is the familiar linear sequence that moves the story along. The hermeneutic code gives the dynamics of the text a paradoxical nature by arresting the enigma and keeping it open. The code of actions and the hermeneutic code operate together on the linear level within the constraints of time, but other codes establish connections that are permutable and reversible. The cultural code has to do with common knowledge, the everyday "reality" in

---

6. Tzvetan Todorov, "Structural Analysis of Narrative," 71.

relation to which the subject adapts her- or himself and lives her or his life. The semic code (a seme is the smallest possible semantic component of a word) is involved in "naming" persons, places, and objects. The reader transforms sentences of a text into semes or qualities of a person under consideration in the process of reading. "If we are told that Sarrasine (a character in a little-known novella of Balzac) had *'one of those strong wills that know no obstacle,'* what are we to read? *will, energy, obstinacy, stubbornness,* etc.?" Barthes says that the naming of the semes is the essence of the reader's activity: "to read is to struggle to name, to subject the sentences of a text to a semantic transformation."[7]

The naming of the seme is erratic. In the semantic transformation of the text, the reader will hesitate among several qualities. The symbolic code, however, is the major code allowing for multivalence and reversibility. Barthes sees this operating through antithesis. When a text sets out two items as oppositions, the reader is enabled to develop a vast symbolic structure involving substitutions and variations in an attempt to join the two antithetic terms or to "affect the inexpiable."[8]

The reader has the task of decomposing the text that is composed of the various codes. In the process, the text is first of all cut up into lexias, textual spaces where meaning can be observed. The lexia may include one word, a few words, or several sentences. The size of the lexia is determined by the reader in the process of reading. The aim of the decoding for Barthes is not the determination of a final denotation. Just as there is no narrative structure, grammar, or logic that serves as the base of the text, there is no final denotation. Reading does not result in a final synthesis of the codes.

The emphasis of the narratologists on the logic or grammar of narrative in general seems to be at odds with Barthes's stance in regard to the reader's involvement and a plurality of meanings. There may be no essential contradiction here, however. Barthes, indeed, comes to his later emphasis on the plurality of meanings from an earlier concern with the constraints of narrative. Such things as the logic of the four-term model remain as the horizon against which the plurality of meaning is emphasized. Jonathan Culler is convinced that the approaches of

7. Roland Barthes, *S/Z*, 3, 92.
8. Ibid., 27.

Greimas and Barthes are not in contradiction. Barthes focuses upon the reader and the process of organizing the text according to the principle of expectation. The ultimate logic and form, however, are due to the four-term model emphasized by Greimas.[9]

Another disagreement with Barthes grows out of concern for a final denotation or meaning. This is in contrast to Barthes's emphasis upon continued connotation. Barthes's "ideal text" is "a triumphant plural, unimpoverished by any constraint of representation (of imitation)." All texts are not "ideal," of course, but even moderately ideal or plural texts may be appreciated by connotation in Barthes's view. Connotation "is a determination, a relation, an anaphora, a feature which has the power to relate itself to anterior, ulterior, or exterior mentions, to other sites of the texts (or of another text)." This relating must not be restrained. Connotation is not to be confused with mere association of ideas. Connotation is a correlation imminent in the text. Denotation, however, is important for Barthes, even though it is an illusion and "no more than the *last* of the connotations." It is the supposedly different systems of denotation and connotation that "enable the text to operate like a game, each system referring to the other according to the requirements of a certain illusion."[10] Here again, it may be suggested that there is no essential contradiction between the connotation and plurality of meanings emphasized by Barthes and the denotation and desire for truth. In the reconciliation of the apparently irreconcilable perspectives, each must be seen as existing only in relation to the other. The play of connotations depends upon the reader's ability to synthesize and find denotation. The possibility of denotation, on the other hand, depends on the ability to analyze and imagine various connotations.

TEXT PROCESSING

"Text processing" or "discourse processing" is a group of movements that provides tools for understanding the process of reading and interpretation. The emphasis on "processing" rather than "analysis" makes clear the perspective of contemporary scholars in the field that the

9. Jonathan Culler, "Defining Narrative Units," 139.
10. Barthes, *S/Z*, 5, 8–9.

reader is an active participant in the actualization of the literary text. Nevertheless, studies less concerned with the process of reading and interpretation as such and more concerned with scientific analysis of the text as a self-contained unit have been influential in text-processing studies. Another distinction is sometimes made—between reception and processing. When a distinction is made, "reception" designates activities in the actualization of a literary text and "processing" refers to what is done with the result of the reception.

In Europe, much early work assumed the possibility of reducing the literary text (the linguistic or literary unit beyond the sentence) to linguistics. The work of Janos S. Petöfi, for example, is rigorously linguistic in its foundations. Götz Wienold begins from a literary perspective with concern for the procedures followed by the participant in literature in the production of new texts (including interpretations) on the basis of an original text. He is not concerned with the reception of texts in the narrow sense. Siegfried S. Schmidt combines both perspectives in his work. After an introduction to the increasing complexity of the components in text processing, the work of these three men will be explicated as representative of the total movement. Then an important aspect of American text processing will be considered.

Components in Text Processing

Scholars involved in text- or discourse-processing studies have provided helpful ways of conceptualizing the components of the total universe of literary interpretation and the ways these components are related to each other. The developments in text-processing studies have paralleled the developments in early formalist-structuralist literary criticism: there was an early concentration on the text itself, seen as a structural whole, then there was a progressive enlargement of the field of the study which, nevertheless, did not mean abandonment of the early structuralist perspective.

Linguistic approaches to the text. In an early period, it was assumed that the structures imminent in the text could be discovered in abstraction from the author, the reader, and the relationships of the text to the world by an approach based on the structural linguistics of Saussure. The relationships of similarity, opposition, and contrast that defined elements on the level of the phoneme and sentence were extended to other linguistic levels and to the level of the text.

The "reduction" of literature to linguistics was greatly encouraged by the development of the generative grammar of Noam Chomsky. "Grammar" refers to the system of morphology, syntax, and phonology that underlies a language and makes possible grammatical sentences of a language. In an early period, Chomsky saw the grammatical system as involving a set of "rules" governing the structure of sentences, a set of "rules" governing transformations of sentences (as changes from active to passive), and a set of "rules" that tell how the sentence as a whole is to be pronounced. Linguistics began to be characterized by ordered rules instead of by the conventional diagrams. And, perhaps more important, the concept of transformation allowed the linguists to conceive of language in a different way than descriptive linguistics. In a later period, Chomsky introduced the idea of linguistic competence by postulating that native speakers of a language master a system of rules which allows them to distinguish grammatical from ungrammatical sentences.

The application of Chomsky's generative grammar in literature took the form of an attempt to develop a text grammar; that is, to develop a grammar that deals with linguistic objects beyond the sentence. Thus, the development of text grammars resulted from seeing a literary text as a specific type of linguistic object with specific psychosocial functions. The conditions, rules, and functions that determine the generation of literary texts were seen as capable as specification just as the rules of determining the generation of sentences.

Beyond linguistics. The assumption that the literary object could be abstracted from author, reader, and world allowed early studies to limit attention to the text. But this assumption was dealt a serious blow by the inability of the various grammars to explain the text in isolation from at least some of these factors. Semantics could not be contained within the relationship of elements within the text; semantics also involves "reference." The "textual" component in literary theory and grammar required a "contextual" component. This did not mean the abandonment of the grammar; it meant that grammar would be a component of a more comprehensive theory of linguistic interaction.

The extension (and relativizing) of grammatical models of literary texts was facilitated by speech-act theory that saw the text not only as a series of sentences but also as a series of speech acts. Communication was seen as involving not only the acts of saying something (locutionary acts) but also acts that have a certain force in saying something (illocutionary acts) and acts that achieve certain results by saying something (perlocutionary acts).

Pragmatic aspects of literary communication reintroduced the question of the author's motivation, sincerity, and strategy. These matters could be related (even reduced) to textual meaning, and/or textual meaning and speaker's meaning could be compared and contrasted. The perlocutionary acts of speech-act theory reintroduced the role of the reader; this role was highlighted by the introduction of "affective" stylistics and considerations of the general theory of reading. S. R. Levin indicates that with this move the heuristics of interpretation came to be emphasized, "the moves, starts, and hypotheses made and developed by the reader in his active processing of the text." The significance of this approach was that the reader brought everything that she or he was and knew to bear on the activity of interpreting of the text.[11]

In progress from structural linguistics through text-linguistics and general semantics into pragmatics, a view of the process of reading and interpretation and even of the text itself developed that contrasted sharply with earlier approaches to text analysis. The progressive enlargement and extension of the model from a linguistic or grammatical form to more comprehensive forms, however, does not mean that scholars abandoned the goal of empirical and logically consistent analysis and interpretation. Levin says that "the text itself . . . continues to be considered for its internal structure" even though "the relations found to pertain therein are no longer regarded as self-sufficient; they are seen, rather, as intentional projections of the author, interpreted constructs of the reader, and semantic mappings onto possible worlds."[12]

Janos S. Petöfi

Petöfi has been involved with text-theoretical problems since 1966—until 1969 in Budapest, from 1969 to 1971 in Göteborg, then in

11. S. R. Levin, "On the Progress of Structural Poetics," 514–15.
12. Ibid., 515.

West Germany. Two major periods can be distinguished in Petöfi's work—the period up to the end of 1972 during which he attempted to formulate a text grammar based on a Chomsky-type sentence grammar and the period since 1972 when he expanded the conceptualization to include extensional semantic interpretation, text production, and text reception. In this last stage, the text-grammar component was united with a contextual-nongrammatical component. The comprehensive text theory is called the "text-structure world-structure theory" and is the framework within which different text-processing operations (analysis, interpretation, synthesis, comparison, or paraphrasing) are carried out. The text-structure world-structure theory is one that is designed to enable the grammatical description of texts and the assigning of meanings (extensional semantic interpretation) to the grammatically described text. In this later work, Montague grammar (which extends the scope of generative grammar to include logico-semantic and formal pragmatics) became more important for the development of a system for text processing. Four specific tasks are outlined in the text-structure world-structure theory:

1. The assigning of (all possible) syntactic (intensional-semantic) representations to natural language texts;
2. The world-semantic (extensional-semantic) interpretation of the individual intensional-semantic representations;
3. The generating of syntactic (intensional-semantic) representations; and
4. The comparing of a text, of the intensional-semantic representation of a text, and of the extensional-semantic representations of a text with other texts, the intensional-semantic representations of other texts, and the extensional-semantic representation of other texts, respectively.[13]

The basic elements of Petöfi's theory are the grammatical component, the extensional-semantic (or world-semantic) component, and the lexicon. The grammatical component is a co-textual component that includes not only grammatical rules but also non-grammatical formal criteria that can be formulated in rules. (The stylistic, poetic, and rhetorical criteria referring to rhyme, rhythm, verse, and other structures are seen by Petöfi as nongrammatical but verbally formal criteria.) The extensional-semantic (world-semantic) component is a

---

13. Janos S. Petöfi, "A Formal Semiotic Text Theory as an Integrated Theory of Natural Language," 38.

contextual component. By contextual, Petöfi means all aspects that are not grammatical or verbally formal. These include not only the extensional-semantic interpretation but also text production and perception. The lexicon contains syntactic and semantic information and is involved in operations in both the grammatical and extensional-semantic components.

Petöfi has developed a model of analysis proceeding from the linear text manifestation to world semantic "representations" and logical and semantic inferences.[14] The initial operations take place in the grammatical component with the assistance of the lexical component. The basic goal is the structural description of the text. Three important operations in the grammatical component are analysis, synthesis, and paraphrasing. Analysis takes place not only on the level of sentences but also on the level of the total text. Sentence-level analysis is designed to assign to sentences their abstract logical bases. The analyzed sentences are considered to be linear manifestations resulting from "deeper" logical foundations. In the process, incomplete sentences are completed; homony is observed; pro-type reference elements (pronouns, for example) are replaced by the original (nouns in the case of pronouns); and arguments are characterized as definite, indefinite, general, etc. Text-level analysis has to do with the structure of the whole of the text. The task of text-level analysis is the assigning of a "macro-structure" that will account for the text-surface representation (the linear arrangement) and the deeper nonlinear representation. In both cases, what is sought is a higher-order unit that can account for the existence of the whole text instead of simply the individual sentences.

Synthesis involves the generation of a text representation. In the scientific approach of Petöfi, such a representation is denoted by a mathematical formula or algorithm. The algorithm is such that the particular linear manifestation of the text will be seen as derived from the representation through transformations.

The operation of paraphrasing (formation of a text not identical with the original) represents a combination of the operations of analysis and

14. Janos S. Petöfi, "Towards an Empirically Motivated Grammatical Theory of Verbal Texts."

synthesis. Analysis attaches a text representation to a given text and synthesis derives from this text representation at least one text that is not the same as the original.

The structural description obtained in grammatical operations is used in the extensional-semantic interpretation whose object is "the relation between the world manifested by the verbal structure and the actual world." The grammar makes it possible to "reveal the 'world' manifesting itself in a text." The world-semantic component is involved in the "interpretation" or "further interpretation" of this text world, that is "the assigning of an *extensional interpretation* to it (and its possible comparison with (an) other world(s))."[15]

The "actual world" with which the world of the text is compared depends upon the nature of the text. With legal texts, there is concern with the problem of "how the 'world of a juridical fact' is made up by different elements (e.g., evidences, statements, records, etc.) and with the relation existing between this world and the 'world manifesting itself in juridical norms or an admissible interpretation of them.'" Among other things theology deals with the problem of "how certain types of sacral texts 'constitute' the 'world which has been fixed in the dogmas' and which relation this world has to the 'actual world' of the simultaneously existing epoch and of the different single epochs, respectively." The theory of literature is concerned with the relationship existing between the "world manifested by the text" and the "actual world" existing at the time of the production or reception of the text.[16]

The relationship between the world of the text and the actual world and hence between the grammatical and world-semantic components differs on the basis of the type of text. With mathematical texts (where the lexicon can be made completely axiomatic), the world-semantic operations are completely defined through the grammatical operations. Literary texts, on the other hand, form a completely free system. The lexicon is a combination of the everyday lexicon and the lexicons of various special areas. The use of metaphor allows a freedom of world-semantic operations that does not exist with other types of text. It

15. Ibid., 272.
16. Ibid., 225–26.

is even possible for the formal elements (rhyme, rhythm, verse form, grammatical parallels, etc.) to be used in world-semantic operations in ways not grounded at all in the grammatical operations. Religious texts, in the opinion of Petöfi, can be interpreted with almost the same degree of freedom as literary texts.

The freedom and openness of literary texts (as compared with mathematical texts, for example) suggest the basic problem of a unidirectional model for analysis of such texts. It is the problem of the construction of a "transformation component" that can bridge the co-textual morphological structure and the contextual logical structure. The problems (whether seen as technical or logical) do not negate the value of such attempts for the scholar interested in the process of reading and interpretation. Even though it must be recognized that components and operations at the world-semantic level affect components at the text-semantic level, the process of reading and interpretation may be conceptualized provisionally as movement from the linear level of manifestation by means of operations in the text-grammatical component to interpretation at the world-semantic level. Processes such as synthesis, analysis, comparison, and paraphrasing, and the maintaining of coherence in the co-textual and contextual components are certainly involved in reading and interpretation. Even though intuition cannot be excluded by development of formal methods, the intuitive operations can be made more explicit and linguistic and logical operations can be seen as accompanying and helping the intuitive hermeneutical operations.

I would suggest that the various "components" in Petöfi's conceptualization may be translated into operations that are necessary for processing texts but the operations cannot be seen simply as unidirectional. The nature of the text as a linear manifestation, composed of linguistic and literary units progressively increasing in size and relationships, makes a unidirectional procedure of text processing theoretically conceivable (at a formal or abstract level). The content or the semantics (at least of literary and religious texts), the meaning of which extends to universes limited only by human cognitive and affective potentiality, cannot be contained and processed in this unidirectional fashion. There must be movement in both directions at the same time.

Götz Wienold

The text-processing concept of Götz Wienold developed as a method of study opposed to the sociological conception of literary communication that reduces literature to communication between author and reader (or audience). A theoretical distinction may be made between the reception of texts and the processing of texts. Wienold is concerned with the processing that follows reception. He says this reformulation of texts is "the essential form by means of which readers and listeners participate in the system of interconnection of texts in a society." "Texts are commented on, praised and criticized, recommended and dismissed, publicized and plagiarized; they are rephrased by words or by means of other media of communication; one assigns meanings to them as well as values and puts them on reading lists."[17]

In Wienold's view, the text-processing model promises a new and productive orientation of *scientific* literary activity because the reformulation of given texts into new texts can be observed and studied scientifically. He begins with the scientific objective of "providing the study of literature with an observable body of events." In order to quantify the study of literature, he identifies literature with text processing and isolates the specific processes involved. By text processing, he means "any process which by taking reference to a text or group of texts produces a new text." Text-processing relations are "the relationships obtaining between the texts forming the beginning and end points of such text processing." With the model of study developed, Wienold is able to compare initiate texts with resultant texts to determine the modes of reference used in text processing.[18] In a study of newspaper criticism, Wienold discovered the following modes of reference: quoting (paraphrasing), condensing, referentializing, giving a metatextual description, evaluating, and justifying. In the analysis of a text of literary criticism, Wienold finds each of these modes used in complex fashions. In one sentence of a "resultant text" several modes may be used. Moreover, the reference to the initiate text is not always made in a direct fashion.

---

17. Götz Wienold, "The Concept of Text Processing, the Criticism of Literature and Some Uses of Literature in Education," 111.
18. Ibid.

Wienold finds a mode of reference in literary criticism that goes beyond the modes observed in newspaper criticism: the "assignment of meaning." This is not a simple mode; it exploits other modes of reference. It is also accomplished by considering the history of processing prior to the processing then taking place.

Wienold's empirical approach moves away from the body of texts called literature to the participants in literature. The participant is the one involved in text processing. Objectives in literature are seen in terms of the participant. The objective in the teaching of literature should be

> not only in terms of being able to perform certain operations one is directed to but in terms of understanding and evaluating such operations. . . . Rather than falling prey to the mandarins of literary criticism and the pythias of interpretation, a student who learns to perform, to analyse and to evaluate text processing may direct himself towards future text processings. He even may come to understand that he is not in need of a criticism or an interpretation, that he may devise specific meaning assignments for specific purposes of his own.[19]

Siegfried J. Schmidt

Schmidt's work results from an attempt to steer a path between a positivistic text-grammar approach and a hermeneutical approach that claims "understanding" as a transcendent operation preceding scientific operations. He terms his approach an empirical literary science and seeks to establish it on the basis of a modern scientific theory. In an early period, the critical rationalism of Karl Popper was used as the basis. Later, the basis became the analytical theory of science proposed by Josef E. Sneed whereby the empirical nature of a statement is not to be decided in "relation to reality as such " but "in relation to a model of reality consensually adopted by a community of investigators."[20]

Schmidt regards as an "uncontested fact" that literary knowledge is based on a great many presuppositions. But he accepts this fact not as a ground for being content with an intuitive approach but as stimulus for a systematic investigation of the presuppositions and an attempt to make them intersubjectively explicit.[21]

19. Ibid., 127.
20. Siegfried J. Schmidt, *"Empirische Literaturwissenschaft* as Perspective," 560.
21. Siegfried J. Schmidt, "On a Theoretical Basis for a Rational Science of Literature," 256.

The acceptance of a scientific theory does not mean that Schmidt feels that *participation* in literature is essentially an objective and scientific enterprise. On the level of participation, subjectivity and value judgments are involved. It is on the level of analysis of the literary process that scientific and objective criteria are important. Schmidt carefully situates the theory of literary communication (including theories of literary production, mediation, reception, and processing) within a theory of aesthetic communication. The theory of aesthetic communication, however, is set within a general theory of communication that is part of a more comprehensive theory of human interaction.[22]

The setting of the theory of literary communication within a theory of aesthetic communication dictates that the meaning sought is polyvalent. In nonaesthetic communication, conventions are oriented toward questions of truth, reference, and usefulness, and scientific methodology requires sanctions against individuals who transgress bounds of the models of reality and usefulness accepted by the group. In aesthetic communication, however, new and creative aims and criteria for activities are introduced and promoted. The polyvalence convention in aesthetic communication increases the possibilities for recipients to assign meaningful and personally relevant structures to literary texts. This convention optimizes reception processes by combining modes of experiencing in one and the same reception process.

The context of the theory of literature within a theory of communication and action allows Schmidt to emphasize the *actor* in the process (individuals, groups of individuals, or institutions) who possesses ability, need, motivation, and intention and who takes actions (concrete, social phenomena) in a given situation. The activity of the actor in the situation of communication is the production of a material means for communication. The text itself, however, is not the object of study for the theory of literature. The text is a communication base by means of which actors construct another material means for communication. This is termed *Kommunikat* by Schmidt. The primary research object, then, is the *Kommunikat*. (It might be helpful to recall the distinction between a text and its concretization in the work of scholars like Ingarden.)[23]

---

22. Siegfried J. Schmidt, *Grundriss der Empirischen Literaturwissenschaft*, 1:19–20.
23. Ibid., 92–109.

Two different procedures are seen by Schmidt: the reception of literary *Kommunikats* and the processing of these *Kommunikats*. The basic postulate supporting reception is the principle of "sense constancy." H. Hormann, who developed the principle as part of a "variable-course-model" of analysis, says that "making sense" or "having sense" is a state accepted as given. "We expect what we hear to make sense, and we analyze the incoming message so as to conform to this criterion. The course and kind of analysis we apply is geared to the goal of making (or keeping) sense."[24] The "variable-course-model" of analysis is in opposition to a "fixed-course-model" moving from syntactic analysis to semantic analysis. In the variable-course-model, the course of analytical operation is altered whenever necessary in order to make sense.

The sense-making by the individual involves co-textual, contextual, and individual factors. All of these are involved in the assignment of a structure to the text which may be seen as a model of the text. Although Schmidt finds a division of the reception process into different levels or parts purely theoretical, this division is helpful for analysis of the process.

The beginning of the process of reception is the perception of the text by the recipient. In the process, the reader assigns a graphic structure to the text. (Schmidt says this is to be distinguished from the text itself. In the process, the reader will omit and overlook certain items, for example.) The next level of operation is postulated as the reader's identification of the perceived elements of the graphic structure as elements from the repertoire of a natural language. The elements are then arranged in a definite structure. When the elements can be assigned to different structures, the reader must choose one of the possible structures. That is, syntactic and semantic ambiguity must be handled by the reader. She or he unites and organizes the data by establishing relationships between the textual elements and by bringing the information into a relationship with structures of knowledge in the memory as well as with information received from the reception situation. The process is successful if the reader knows to which frame

24. H. Hormann, "The Concept of Sense Constancy," 5. Cited in S. J. Schmidt, *Grundriss* 1:245.

of reference the intentions of the textual elements can be assigned and in which macrostructure (the overall structure, a global-meaning structure) they can be organized.

Schmidt says the entire process of reception is marked by anticipation and correction. That is, the reader forms certain expectations that influence the reception and in the process these expectations are modified and corrected. Expectations have to do with the syntactic category to which the next word in a sentence can belong, the textual elements that can occur in a position in question, the probability of the occurrence of linguistic expressions in definite contexts, the regularities of conversation that have come to be expected on the basis of early experience, probabilities that are related to the reader's system of assumptions, and the sort of speech-act involved in communication.[25]

Schmidt summarizes the process of reception as follows: The act of reception begins with the perception of a text and its decoding. The receiver then assigns to the perceived structure an emotionally colored cognitive structure as meaning. In this process she or he makes use of cultural rules of meaning in order to assign a *Kommunikat* coherent to the receiver. These rules have to do with the elimination of syntactic and semantic ambiguity, anticipation and correction, construction of macrostructures through the use of macrorules, making inferences, attaching intentions to extralinguistic correlates, attachment of intentions to frames of reference. The reader can assign additional senses to the perceived structure by generating relationships between the cognitive structure assigned to the perceived structure and elements of the linguistic systems of assumption and the linguistic situation of communication.[26]

Schmidt distinguishes text-processing procedures from reception procedures. The *Kommunikats* that result from reception are used in processing. Processing operations are intentional acts of participants in literary communication designed to produce texts that can play a role as thematic *Kommunikats* in literary communication. The basic operation in processing is that of *Kommunikat*-verbalization, the result of which

25. S. J. Schmidt, *Grundriss* 1:248.
26. Ibid., 265.

is called a *Kommunikat* report. In addition to the basic verbalization of *Kommunikats*, Schmidt discusses condensation (a reduction of the text by means of ordering the series of propositions to a macrostructure), metatextual descriptions (which assign a statement to one element or to the totality of a *Kommunikat* report), evaluation (formulation of normative statements), and clarification (formulation of hypotheses that function to satisfy the needs of a group of participants in communication).[27]

In his discussion of text-processing operations and results, Schmidt acknowledges that descriptive, explanatory, and valuative statements have their place in a theory of literary communication. Schmidt, therefore, sees the need for interpretation. The enormous expansion of literary production since the eighteenth century and the discrepancy between the literary ideas of the public and literary critics has led to the need for competent participants to clarify how a definite literary work is to be read, understood, and evaluated. Psychic needs are also met through interpretation—the need to coordinate our sense data into recurrent structures and to form satisfying conceptual and emotional systems. When an individual confronts a linguistic object that presents difficulties, the individual seeks to solve the problem and produce a coherent *Kommunikat*. This search for coherence that is carried out on the level of the receiver in literary communication can be defined as a function that assigns propositions, inferences, associations, emotions, and values to a text until a recipient has a feeling that she or he has discerned the text and the details of the text, classified the text in conceptual and functional structures, and related her or his emotional response to the text.[28]

For Schmidt, this process of interpretation should not be confused with the assigning of a "correct" meaning to a text. The aesthetic and polyvalence conventions rule out the goal of the "correct" meaning or *the* meaning that is adequate for the author's intention. Statements growing out of complex processing procedures are not judged on the basis of the effective mediation of correct meaning but on the basis of their logically correct argumentation, their empirical validity, and their

27. Ibid., 383–84.
28. Ibid., 293–94, 300.

fruitfulness in solving new problems. The need that Schmidt attempts to meet in his theory of literary communication, then, is not the need met by interpretation. It is not the need to establish a consensus that satisfies a group of readers. It is a need to satisfy empirical demands. Schmidt's work may prove helpful, not by reducing our participation in literature to the scientific level he envisions, but by utilizing the insights he explicates in our reading and interpretation.

Text Processing in American Studies: Schema Theory

Studies in text- or discourse-processing in the American context have paralleled developments in Europe. They have grown out of the scientific study of the structure of language beginning with the sound system and extending to morphology, single sentences, and multisentence discourse. The study of discourse in particular has involved not only linguistic structures and internal semantic relationships but also extralinguistic relationships. Volumes edited by Roy O. Freedle contain articles from numerous perspectives illustrating activities on the American scene. The areas include sociolinguistics, psycholinguistics, ethnomethodology and the sociology of language, educational psychology (teacher-student interaction), philosophy of language, and computational linguistics. No organizing principle can be seen in the various articles in the first volume; in the second volume, schema theory is seen as a theoretical orientation that can serve as organizer of the complex field.[29] Schemata (as observed in the previous chapter) are conceptual frames that provide the basis for interpreting data at various levels of the text.

The notion of schema is not new. The term itself goes back at least to Immanuel Kant, who proposed that the experiences of people are collected together in memory and that common elements of these collected experiences identify categories of experience and allow the synthesis of abstract knowledge to represent the category. The higher-order concept can be understood apart from reference to any specific occurrence within the category, and experiences of the category may be identified by reference to the general schema that describes the

---

29. Roy O. Freedle, "Introduction," *New Directions in Discourse Processing*, xiii.

category.[30] Contemporary schema theory provides a vocabulary and a conceptual framework for the representation of what occurs in the processing of texts. As a scientific theory, it has been criticized because of its weakness as a predictive theory. That is, schema theory "is able to explain *post hoc* virtually any set of available data." The difficulty is not that certain data are inconsistent with schema theory; the problem is that "it is difficult to find any data that are *inconsistent*" with it.[31] The limitations of schema theory as a strictly scientific theory do not limit its usefulness as a heuristic device for a reader-centered theory of textual processing, however. Indeed schema theory becomes transformed when applied to a reader-centered view of text processing, or perhaps more accurately, the scientific limitations of schema theory are seen as a description of the actual hermeneutical situation. The textual data themselves cannot dictate one meaning because dynamic extratextual realities always provide guidance in textual processing. Schemata, or conceptual frames that provide the basis for interpreting data, are necessary at all levels of the text. Schema theory, therefore, is opposed to the view of reading as a series of processes organized hierarchically from single-letter recognition on through higher levels. In the hierarchical bottom-up view, the effects of higher-order processes are seen as null in relation to lower-order processes. The awareness of readers' use of schemata reverses this view. Higher-order processes facilitate lower-order processing. Schema theory emphasizes that in reading a meaningful passage, one is not reading the letters, words, and sentences in the passage as they would be read in isolation. The skilled reader, in fact, does not find it necessary to struggle with every graphemic detail of the writing but processes lower-order information only as is necessary to complete or check on higher-order schemata or hypotheses about the content of the passage. A schema-theoretical approach sees a text as providing directions for readers to construct the meaning from their own knowledge.

The basic schema-theoretical conceptualization of reading is bottom-up processing of incoming data on the basis of top-down schema

---

30. Perry W. Thorndyke and Frank R. Yekovich, "A Critique of Schema-based Theories of Human Story Memory," 25.
31. Ibid., 40.

processing. Schemata provide the context and content within which underlying components and elements can be understood. For example, the mention of "a counter" in an account where the conceptual schema is "going to a restaurant" calls to mind not an abacus or a parrying boxer's blow but a place where food is served. Top-down and bottom-up processing occur at the various levels of reading simultaneously. Through bottom-up processing, utilizing the best-fitting schemata, the incoming data enters the system. The information is processed upward through increasingly comprehensive levels of schemata and interpretation. The top-down processing occurs as the system searches for information to satisfy the previously established top-level schema or the reader's conceptual set.

Marilyn Jager Adams and Allan Collins describe the actual process of reading a text at the word level:

> The eye collects information about different visual features that are present. These are features that are automatically bound to slots that they fit in the letter schemata. Meanwhile, partially instantiated letter schemata are trying to find the appropriate visual features to fill their remaining slots. In addition, they are facilitating other letter schemata that correspond to likely neighbors and, finally, fitting themselves to slots in the word schemata. While all of this is happening, partially activated word schemata are trying to identify the appropriate letters for their own unfilled slots.[32]

Parallel with word processing is sentence and story processing at the syntactic and semantic levels. Words are seeking sentences, and sentences are seeking words; sentences are seeking stories, and stories are seeking sentences. Just as the reader's conceptualization of the constitution of letters and words plays a part in word recognition, the reader's conceptualization of the constitution of sentences and stories plays a part in the processing at the higher levels.

The interpretative level involves story processing but it goes beyond simply following the story. At this level, the reader imposes a structure on the total passage that involves her or his perception of the author's intentions and/or the reader's own goals. Schemata at the interpretive level are not simply compelled by the text.

---

32. Marilyn Jager Adams and Allan Collins, "A Schema-Theoretic View of Reading," 12.

In schema theory, it has become evident that some grand-schema must be conceptualized which provides an awareness of purpose that is more comprehensive than any of the schemata of the text. Coherence is maintained by means of this grand-schema. This level has to do with an understanding of the world in general that is beyond the understanding of the text but which is necessarily integrated with the understanding of the text. That is, the grand-schema is not a "given" that can be empirically proven. It has to do with basically unproved and unprovable presuppositions and ideologies or ideals. Nevertheless, the grand-schema must be compatible with the data involved in the bottom-up processing.

THE HISTORY OF RECEPTION AND
EFFECT (IMPACT)

The Aesthetics of Reception:
Hans Robert Jauss

In West German literary study, the Constance School of Hans Robert Jauss and Wolfgang Iser may be credited with making the reader a central factor of the study of literature. The beginning of this emphasis is to be dated to Jauss's inaugural address at the University of Constance in 1967: "What Is and Why Does One Study Literary History?" In the title and text, Jauss associated himself with J. C. F. Schiller (whose inaugural address at Jena at the end of the eighteenth century was entitled "What Is and Why Does One Study Universal History?") and with the progressive form of classical philosophy of history that attempted to link present needs with past history by studying those phenomena which, according to Schiller, "have fundamentally and indisputably influenced the present shape of the world and the condition of today's generation."[33]

Although the address of Jauss has been "enshrined as the origin of modern reception theory" in West German literary criticism,[34] the address did not immediately outline a complete program of literary study to replace conventional approaches. The address consisted of seven

33. Hans Robert Jauss, *Literaturgeschichte als Provokation der Literaturwissenschaft*, 14 n. 19.
34. Henry J. Schmidt, " 'Text-Adequate Concretizations' and Real Readers," 158.

theses that would reorient literary historical methods. The success of Jauss's challenge in generating debate and in stimulating reception studies was due in part to the historical circumstances in which it was issued. The student demands of the 1960s to restructure knowledge and to come immediately to terms with what was being discussed nationally and internationally was an appropriate context, as was the University of Constance itself, a newly formed university organized on an interdisciplinary basis and unburdened by tradition.

The broader context (not to be completely divorced from the immediate context) that helps explain the continuing success of Jauss's basic ideas was that of growing dissatisfaction with prevailing methods. In an article entitled "A Change of Paradigm in Literary Criticism" Jauss himself pictured the broad background of literary studies against which reception aesthetics can be understood. The impulse for a change of paradigm was the failure of the prevailing paradigm and its methodological axioms to provide what literary studies consistently require, which is, according to Jauss, "the capacity to rescue works of art from the past by means of continually new interpretations, to transfer them into a new presence, to make the experience preserved in past art once more available, in other words: to ask questions—which must be discovered by each new generation—questions to which the art of the past can respond for us once again."[35]

Three paradigms are cited by Jauss as having been successful: the normative poetics of humanism and classicism, the literary revolution of the Romantic period including the development of historical philological methods, and the formal method of stylistic criticism and text-intrinsic aesthetics. But these paradigms became exhausted when their methods of interpretation could no longer accomplish the actualization and transformation of past art into the present. Jauss expressed the opinion that a fourth paradigm had not yet replaced the text-intrinsic-formalist method but he declared that a crisis was obvious. According to Jauss, the critical point at which the text-intrinsic paradigm began to stagnate was the recognition by Russian formalism that the work of art must always be perceived against the background of other works of art and through association with those works.

---

35. Hans Robert Jauss, "Paradigmawechsel in der Literaturwissenschaft," 54–55.

In his inaugural address, Jauss presented his challenge in terms of the dispute between the Marxist and formalist schools and declared that his approach "begins at the point at which both schools stop." In formalism the reader is needed "only as a perceiving subject who follows the directions of the text in order to perceive its form or discover its technique of procedure." The Marxist school equates the reader's experience with the scholarly interest of historical materialism; relationships between the economic basis of production and the literary work are sought as part of the intellectual superstructure. In both instances, the true role of the reader is ignored—a role which has aesthetic and historical implications.[36]

Jauss's seven theses are designed to provide a systematic approach to the rewriting of literary history. The first two theses emphasize that the reader's past experience of the "literary data" is the dialogue that creates "the first condition for a literary history."[37] This experience and dialogue are not purely subjective; the textual strategy, overt and hidden signals, familiar characteristics, and implicit allusions predispose readers of a literary work to a definite type of reception.

The third and fourth theses state the value of the reconstruction of the horizon of expectations of a work. The way a work satisfies or fails to satisfy expectations is a criterion for determination of its aesthetic value—for the first readers and for succeeding readers. Reconstruction of the horizon of expectations for later readers enables the discernment of the questions that the text originally answered and the discovery of the understanding of the text according to its intention and its time. The determination of the questions answered by the text originally, however, is always done within history. Jauss relies upon Hans-Georg Gadamer's criticism of historical objectivism to show that "the reconstructed question can no longer be stated in its original context because this historical context is always surrounded by the context of our present."[38]

In his last three theses Jauss looks at the historical relevance of literature (the productive aspects) from three perspectives: diachronic (the ordering of the individual work in its literary series); synchronic (the

36. Hans Robert Jauss, "Literary History as a Challenge to Literary Theory," 7.
37. Ibid., 9.
38. Ibid., 20.

cross-section arrangement of contemporaneous heterogeneous works so as to discover a general system of relationships of literature of one historical moment); and social (the discernment of the effect of the special history of literature from the general history of its readers).

Jauss and the Constance School have expanded the horizon of their studies from a theory of the reception and effect of literature based on a science of the text to a theory of literary communication that must be developed in cooperation with linguistics, semiotics, sociology, anthropology, philosophy, and even biology. Jauss sees as indispensable the step from "a history of works and artistic genres to a history of aesthetic experience, i.e., the producing, receiving and communicating aesthetic activity of man."[39] Reception aesthetics, then, is not seen as an autonomous methodological paradigm, but as a partial methodological reflection that can serve to subject art to the historicality of understanding and to gain for aesthetic experience the lost social and communicative function.

The Aesthetics of Response:
Wolfgang Iser

Although reception theory is associated with Jauss's attempt to rehabilitate literary history (and is to be seen as standing in the Czech tradition of Mukarovsky and Vodicka) the contribution of the Constance School also involves studies of the process by which a reader actualizes a text (to be seen in the hermeneutical tradition but more directly in the phenomenological tradition of Ingarden). This aspect has been stressed by Wolfgang Iser. Iser defines his approach to the reading process as "phenomenological," emphasizing that "in considering a literary work, one must take into account not only the actual text but also, and in equal measure, the actions involved in responding to that text."[40] Iser's concern is to formulate not "a theory of the aesthetics of reception" arising from a history of readers' judgments, but "a theory of aesthetic response" which "has its roots in the text."[41] Although Iser's interest is in "the response-inviting structure of the text," the framework provided by

39. Hans Robert Jauss, "An Interview with Hans Robert Jauss," 90.
40. Wolfgang Iser, "The Reading Process," 274.
41. Wolfgang Iser, *The Act of Reading*, x.

this approach will "permit assessment and evaluation of actual readers' responses to a literary text."[42]

Iser makes the "gaps" and completion of "gaps" by the reader the central factor in literary communication. A text is seen as a system of processes whereby language allows itself to be broken up and reconstituted. The place where language is broken up and reconstituted "is marked by the gaps in the text—it consists in the blanks which the reader is to fill in. . . . Whenever the reader bridges the gap, communication begins. The gaps function as a kind of pivot on which the whole text-reader relationship revolves."[43]

In early articles Iser speaks of gaps existing in different textual elements and on different levels: syntax, semantics, pragmatics, narrative flow, character action, even the role assigned to the reader.[44] The process of reading is presented by Iser as establishing connections—filling in the gaps—among and between the different levels and phases of the text. Textual segments such as sentences "make statements, claims, or observations, or convey information, and so establish various perspectives on the text."[45] But the sentences aim at something beyond what is actually said. A process is set in motion by the sentences, a process out of which the actual content of the text emerges. But the connections between the sentence correlates are actually left blank, and for Iser it is the connections or interactions that give sentences their special quality.

The idea of gaps between textual segments in the syntagmatic process is associated with the idea of blanks. The first function of the "gap" or "blank" is to enable segments of the various perspectives of the text to be joined together. In this function, the blank is the empty space between segments. As a result of the joining of these two segments, however, a referential field is formed in which the segments exist in tension. There is need for a common framework that will show the affinities and differences to be grasped as a pattern. The text provides no such framework; it must be created by the reader in an act of ideation.

42. Wolfgang Iser, "Interview," 61.
43. Iser, *Act of Reading*, 169.
44. Iser, "The Reading Process," "Indeterminacy and the Reader's Response in Prose Fiction," and "The Reality of Fiction: A Functionalist Approach to Literature."
45. Iser, "The Reading Process," 277.

It is as if the blank in the field of the reader's viewpoint has changed its position. It began as the empty space between segments, indicating . . . their 'connectability,' and so organizing them into projections of reciprocal influence. But with the establishment of this 'connectability' the blank, as the unformulated framework of these interacting segments, now enables the reader to produce a determinant relationship between them.[46]

The "most decisive" function of the blank is not the connecting of the segments or the discernment of the totality of the structure of the referential field of segments. It has to do with the switching of viewpoints between the perspective segments in the process of reading. A segment on which the viewpoint is focused at a particular time is the "theme." When the focus is switched to another segment, the new segment becomes the theme and the earlier segment loses its thematic relevance. The earlier segment, then, is a blank, or a vacancy. These vacancies, however, "are important guiding devices for building up the aesthetic object, because they condition the reader's view of the new theme, which in turn conditions his view of previous themes."[47]

The process of filling the blanks between segments and processing segments in a theme-and-horizon order is a syntagmatic process. Related to the syntagmatic process is a blank on the paradigmatic axis that is also vital for the reader's relationship to the text. The blank on the paradigmatic axis is the result of the negation of the norms of the familiar world that are introduced into the text by means of the repertoire. A text contains references to earlier works, expressions of social and historical norms, and evidence of the culture from which the text has emerged. A specific external reality has been incorporated into the text, a reality that "offers the reader a definite frame of reference or invokes a definite range of past experience." In the literary work, however, the norms have been removed from an original context and set in a new context. In the original context the reader is unaware of them as norms, but in the new context the reader may become aware of them as norms. The reader "has the chance to perceive consciously a system in which he had hitherto been unconsciously caught up, and his awareness will be all the greater if the validity of these norms is negated." The blank created by negation on the

46. Iser, *Act of Reading*, 198.
47. Ibid.

paradigmatic level is filled when the reader adopts attitudes "through which the text can actually be experienced by the reader."[48] Iser sees a "basic force in literary communication" that is more comprehensive than the gaps and blanks on the syntagmatic and paradigmatic levels. This basic force is the "frame" within which the relevant textual material is organized and subsumed. He speaks of this force as "negativity," a reality to be experienced and not explained. "If we were able to explain its effect, we would have mastered it discursively and we would have rendered obsolescent the experience it provides." Nevertheless, this negativity can be partially defined and some important features explained. In essence, negativity is the unformulated "double" or "background" to which "practically all the formulations of the text refer." Negativity is "the unwritten base" that conditions the formulations of the text by way of blanks and negation. It is "the reverse side of the represented world."[49]

In terms of communication, negativity is "an enabling structure." But it is a structure or a frame that is unformulated and must be "built up into a coherent whole by the reader's process of ideation."[50] In the formulation of the cause underlying the questioning of the world in the text, the reader must transcend that world. The reader's formulation of negativity enables an observation of the world from outside. In Iser's opinion, the true communicatory function of literature lies in this activity.

The view of reading advocated by Iser results in a reconceptualization of the meaning of a literary text—meaning is an effect to be experienced, and the meaning of the effectiveness depends upon the participation of the reader. The literary text offers a perspective or view of the world through a system of perspectives that shade into each other and converge on a "general meeting place" which can be called "the meaning of the text." This convergence is not stated or represented in the literary text. It is dependent upon a standpoint that is also lacking in the text. The reader's role is prestructured by the different perspectives (given in the text), the vantage point (from which the reader joins the perspective),

48. Ibid., 212, 217.
49. Ibid., 225, 226, 229.
50. Ibid., 226.

and the point of convergence. The role prescribed by the text and the reader's own disposition operate together with the structure of the text allowing different ways of fulfilling the process. "The process of fulfillment is always a selective one, and any one actualization can be judged against the background of the others potentially present in the textual structure of the reader's role."[51]

The conventional view of interpretation emphasizes explanation with meaning as an object to be defined. Conventional criticism makes a division between subject (the reader) and object (the meaning), with the subject defining the meaning in relation to particular frames of reference. "The criterion for the truthfulness of the definition" in fact is taken to be the fact that the frame is independent of the subject. Traditional interpretive styles need a system that can set literary objects in a symmetrical picture. This is seen by Iser as an elementary stage of the aesthetic impulse that breaks down when the reader has "inwardly become equal to the significance of the object." At that point, the context of other objects is not needed for derivation of the significance of the literary object. The consistency building that Iser emphasizes as a part of the reading process is not a consistency derived or justified merely from classical norms that require harmony between the different elements. The consistency building Iser advocates has to do with "a structure of comprehension" that depends on the reader and not the work. It allows for meaning that rises out of the process of actualization.[52]

51. Ibid., 10, 37.
52. Ibid., 9, 18.

CHAPTER 4

The American Context

Reader-oriented literary approaches in America represent positive responses to different waves of influence from the European context. These responses have been characterized as "a multiplicity of crisscrossing, often divergent tracks that cover a vast area of the critical landscape in a pattern whose complexity dismays the brave and confounds the faint of heart."[1] Indeed, it often seems as if the entire critical landscape is an armed camp made up of a multitude of "iconoclastic" reader-oriented theories and approaches on the one side with an equal number of determined and vociferous opponents on the other. According to Frank Lentricchia, this has resulted in the critical theory of recent decades being the "most confusing" and "richest" in our critical history.[2]

The major contemporary challenge to conventional approaches in America consists of critics who have appropriated ideas of Jacques Derrida. This chapter will begin, then, by describing the work of Derrida and his American disciples. Then the defense by E. D. Hirsch of "stable determinacy of meaning" against "dogmatic relativists" or "cognitive atheists" will be drawn. This chapter will also treat the rhetorical approach that sees the reader as a textual reality (with the actual reader carrying out the features dictated by the author) and psychoanalytic-oriented theories that relate meaning to the personality

---

1. Susan R. Suleiman, "Introduction: Varieties of Audience-Oriented Criticism," 6.
2. Frank Lentricchia, *After the New Criticism*, xi.

or identity of the reader. The work of Wayne Booth and Norman Holland serve to illuminate rhetorical and psychoanalytic-oriented approaches.

DERRIDA AND THE AMERICAN DERRIDEANS: DECONSTRUCTION

The Nature of Deconstruction

The method that has served as a focus of attention in most recent American criticism is termed "deconstruction." According to Christopher Norris, deconstruction is "post-structural" in relation to a structuralism that was domesticated and became "just one more available method for saying new things about well-worn texts."[3] In terms of the structuralism imported into America from France in the 1970s, Norris would appear to be correct. Jonathan Culler (whom Norris sees as the individual most responsible for the domestication of structuralism) contrasts in a concise way structuralism and poststructuralism from such a position:

> In simplest terms, structuralists take linguistics as a model and attempt to develop "grammars"—systematic inventories of elements and their possibilities of combinations—that would account for the form and meaning of literary works; post-structuralists investigate the way in which this project is subverted by the workings of the texts themselves. Structuralists are convinced that systematic knowledge is possible; post-structuralists claim to know only the impossibility of this knowledge.[4]

The investigation by poststructuralists of the way that the project of the structuralists "is subverted by the workings of the texts themselves" is responsible for the label "deconstruction." Deconstruction, however, is not merely an intellectual strategy or mode of reading. It is a philosophical position, a challenge by Derrida to "logocentrism" or the "metaphysics of presence." In Western philosophy the nature and reality of things in the universe is grounded in presence. Meaning in human intercourse is taken to be something present to the consciousness of the speaker which is expressed through signs. Meaning is what the

---

3. Christopher Norris, *Deconstruction*, 1.
4. Jonathan Culler, *On Deconstruction*, 22.

speaker had in mind. In the Cartesian "I think, therefore I am," the *I* is present to itself in the act of thinking and is considered beyond doubt.

In speaking, the meaning is mediated directly by the speaker who can control the situation and ensure that the speaker's meaning is conveyed. In writing, however, the speaker cannot do this. Writing, then, is an artificial substitute for speech. The opposition between meaning (or speech which permits relatively direct mediation) and writing is a form of opposition between what is fundamental and something that is a manifestation, between the high presence and a fall. Oppositions such as meaning/form, intelligible/sensible, soul/body, intuition/expression, serious/nonserious, literal/metaphorical, nature/culture, positive/negative, and transcendental/empirical are understood as oppositions between an origin (which is normal, self-identical, simple, intact) and the fall from this origin (complication, derivation, deterioration).

Logocentrism assumes the priority of the first term. Analysis, then, is "the enterprise of returning 'strategically,' in idealization, to an origin."[5] Deconstruction as philosophy points out the flaw in the metaphysics of presence. When particular instances of presence are argued as grounds for further development, the instances cited turn out to be products themselves, dependent and derivative and, therefore, deprived of the authority of pure presence. An examination of the way that words and language itself mean illustrates the difficulties of the metaphysics of presence. It is plausible to conceive of a word as having a meaning that speakers have given it in communication in the past. The system of language is also a result of prior speech acts. It is impossible, however, to reach an originary event not dependent upon prior organization and differentiation. Even if a cavedweller inaugurated language by a speech sound signifying "food," the sound would make sense only because it is distinguished from other sounds. The world must have already been divided into "food" and "nonfood." The differentiations that are involved in communication (whether of the cavedweller or of modern people), however, cannot serve as an originary ground. Differences are not merely given; they are also products. Meaning is a source of language, but meaning is also a product of language. Deconstruction as philosophy does not lead to a theory that does away with this

5. Jacques Derrida, *Limited Inc.*, 236. Quoted in Culler, *On Deconstruction*, 93.

inconsistency. It exposes as untenable theories grounded on presence while utilizing that very theory.[6]

Culler defines and illustrates the intellectual strategy based on the philosophy of deconstruction: "to deconstruct a discourse is to show how it undermines the philosophy it asserts, or the hierarchical oppositions on which it relies, by identifying in the text the rhetorical operations that produce the supposed ground of argument, the key concept or premise."[7] The Nietzschean deconstruction of causality is an instance of the deconstructive process. In the fragments of *The Will to Power*, Friedrich Nietzsche questions the assumptions of the logical and temporal priority of cause in relation to effect. This concept, he argues, is not a given but the product of a chronological reversal. When one feels a pain, a cause is sought. When a pin is discovered, the causal sequence, *pin . . . pain*, is established. In fact, however, "the fragment of the outside world of which we become conscious comes after the effect that has been produced on us and is projected *a posteriori* as its 'cause.' In the phenomenalism of the 'inner world' we invert the chronology of cause and effect. The basic fact of 'inner experience' is that the cause gets imagined after the effect has occurred."[8]

Three implications for the practice of deconstructive criticism are drawn by Culler from Nietzsche's treatment of causality. First, deconstruction of causality does not lead to the conclusion that the principle itself is illegitimate and should be discarded. Indeed, the principle of causation is used in the process of deconstruction of causality. The experience of pain *causes* the discovery of the pin. It causes the production of a cause. Second, the deconstruction of causality does not conclude with skepticism. It is not the same as David Hume's skeptical argument that causation is not demonstrable, that contiguity and temporal succession do not constitute a proof of causation. Deconstruction asserts the indispensability of causation and uses it to deny any rigorous justification to causation. The third point made by Culler is that since the argument which elevates "cause" can also favor "effect," the force of the idea of origin is no longer the same. The loss of

---

6. Culler, *On Deconstruction*, 95–96.
7. Ibid., 86.
8. Friedrich Nietzsche, *Werke*, 3:804. Quoted in Culler, *On Deconstruction*, 86.

the metaphysical privilege of origin disrupts the system which depended upon it.[9]

Use of Deconstruction in Literary Study

The possibility of the use of deconstruction in literary study depends to some degree on the view taken of deconstruction and the capacity of the reader to make sense of that view. It is popular to read Derrida in particular and deconstruction in general as simply denying the role of the author's intention and the conventions of language in favor of a completely free play of meaning. Derrida and deconstruction may be viewed in a different way, however. The view of Derrida simply as a hedonist and deconstruction as an unqualified free play, according to Frank Lentricchia, is a "skewing of Derrida," even if the blame can be placed on Derrida himself for "too much subordinating" of the subthemes and consequences of decentering which would "suggest we might find something more valuable to do than meditate with endless repetition on the bottomless abyss of writing."[10]

Lentricchia highlights tendencies in Derrida that "have the effect of moving us on . . . in order to interrogate, from within writing, and on wholly temporal and cultural grounds, what (if not naked being) does shape and inform the play of signification."[11] To the charge that he was a destroyer (following his delivery of the lecture "Structure, Sign, and Play in the Discourse of the Human Sciences"), for example, Derrida responded: "I didn't say there was no center, that we could get along without the center. I believe that the center is a function, not a being—a reality, but a function. And this function is absolutely indispensable. The subject is absolutely indispensable. I don't destroy the subject; I situate it."[12]

Derrida, in the estimation of Lentricchia, brings to conclusion the project of Nietzsche, defined as the "liberation of the signifier from its dependence or derivation with respect to the logos and the related

---

9. Culler, On Deconstruction, 87–88.
10. Lentricchia, After the New Criticism, 170.
11. Ibid., 171.
12. Jacques Derrida, "Structure, Sign, and Play in the Discourse of the Human Sciences," 271. Quoted in Lentricchia, After the New Criticism, 174.

concept of truth or the primary signified."[13] But he also suggests a new project:

> . . . to uncover the nonontological reincarnation of the signifier within cultural matrices which, though themselves subject to difference and change, nevertheless in their moment of power, use the signifier, take hold of it, establish dominance over it in order to create truth, value, and rationality, and then violently set these *in place* as norms, coercive contexts for expression, meaning, and sanity that claim for themselves externality and universality, even though these norms will themselves be displaced in time by new structures of domination.[14]

This project, subordinated by Derrida himself and overlooked by American Derrideans, must be seen in light of the work of Michel Foucault. Instead of seeing discourse governed from without by some nondiscoursive temporal ground, Foucault sees discourse governed or contextualized by rules that are always subject to historical transformation. Truth and rationality are always confined within historical determinations. It is not enough to speak the truth, Foucault says, one must be "within the truth."[15] If one does not wish to speak truth "in a void," one must place oneself within the systems that determine truth for one's time.

Lentricchia suggests that the subjection of the texts of Derrida and Foucault to deconstruction will result in a positive evaluation of deconstruction: "Our contemporary historicity may perhaps be no more, or less, than the deconstructive project in its strangely divided identity: decadent and phlegmatic, and yet bravely energetic and full of hope; paralytic and corrosively self-ironic, and yet awesomely productive and full of assurance."[16]

Varieties of Deconstruction

The dissolving of the distinction between philosophical and literary texts and the observation of the different ways that philosophical texts undermine philosophy's assumption of its own serious, literal, and

13. Jacques Derrida, *Of Grammatology*, 19. Quoted in Lentricchia, *After the New Criticism*, 175.
14. Lentricchia, *After the New Criticism*, 176.
15. Michel Foucault, *The Archaeology of Knowledge*, 224. Quoted in Lentricchia, *After the New Criticism*, 196–97.
16. Lentricchia, *After the New Criticism*, 210.

truthful nature has characterized contemporary deconstruction. Some critics see this sort of activity as genuine deconstruction and Paul de Man as its foremost American exponent. "De Man's readings draw out the innermost logic of the text, showing how figurative tensions develop to a point where that logic is implicitly confounded by its own implications. For de Man this discrepancy between reason and rhetoric is endemic to all literary texts."[17]

In the final analysis, however, there is a performative aspect of the text or of language that is immune from deconstruction. De Man asserts that to the extent metaphysics or philosophy is "literary," its deconstruction is impossible.[18] Rhetoric in the performative mode escapes the rigors of deconstruction. In the chapters on Rousseau in *Allegories of Reading*, de Man marks the distinction between cognition and action, and notes the primacy of a type of action that is the product not of the author or even the reader but of language. The *Social Contract* is a theoretical description of the state that disintegrates as soon as it is put into motion. The speech act of the text signals toward a hypothetical future in that "all laws are future-oriented and prospective; their elocutionary mode is that of the *promise*." But "every promise assumes a date at which the promise is made and without which it would have no validity; laws are promissory notes in which the present of the promise is always a past with regard to its realization."[19] Rousseau said that the law of today should be an act of today's general will: "We have not committed ourselves to do what the people wanted but what they want. It follows that when the Law speaks in the name of the people, it is in the name of the people of today and not of the past." This is impossible! The situation is hopeless. "The people subject to the law must be the authors of the law."[20] The blind mob cannot promulgate a system of law, yet it must. For this to take place, there must be a reversal of cause and effect. Prior to the laws, human beings must be what they are to become through the laws. Some sort of divine teleological system must be presupposed. The lawgiver must substitute his or her own for the divine voice. This is blasphemous; the *Social Contract* explicitly

17. Norris, *Deconstruction*, 100.
18. Paul de Man, *Allegories of Reading*, 131.
19. Ibid., 273.
20. J. J. Rousseau, *Oeuvres complètes*, 3:316, 390. Quoted in de Man, *Allegories of Reading*, 273, 274.

denies divine inspiration for itself. But this blasphemous deceit is necessary to put the paralysis in motion.

De Man says, then, that Rousseau clearly undermines the authority of his own legislative discourse. De Man calls the *Social Contract* a "metafigural" allegory, "an allegory of a figure . . . which relapses into the figure it deconstructs." It is an allegory of a figure in that it is "indeed structured like an aporia: it persists in performing what it has shown to be impossible to do." The *Social Contract* resorts to the very principle of authority that it undermines.

> That the *Social Contract* denies the right to promise is clear from the fact that the legislator has to invent a transcendental principle of signification called God in order to perform the metalepsis that reverses the temporal pattern for all promissory and legal statements. Since God is said to be, within this perspective, a subterfuge, it follows that the *Social Contract* has lost the right to promise anything yet it promises a great deal.[21]

According to de Man, the reintroduction of the promise is not a result of the discretion of the writer. It is not a result of an inconsistency, a weakness in the text that could have been avoided. The promising is not simply done explicitly in passages that can be isolated; the promising is done more effectively—through inference. The act of promising, the performative efficacy of the text, then,

> is due to the rhetorical model of which it is a version. This model is a fact of language over which Rousseau himself has no control. Just as any other reader, he is bound to misread his text as a promise of political change. The error is not within the reader; language itself dissociates the cognition from the act. *Die Sprache verspricht (sich);* to the extent that it is necessarily misleading, language just as necessarily conveys the promise of its own truth. This is also why textual allegories on this level of rhetorical complexity generate history.[22]

When the linguistic structures are stated in political terms, the incompatibility between grammar and meaning becomes explicit. "Rousseau defines the State or the law as a 'double relationship' that, at close examination turns out to be as self-destructive as it is unavoidable. In the description of the structure of political society, the 'definition' of a

21. De Man, *Allegories of Reading,* 276.
22. Ibid., 277.

text as the contradictory interference of the grammatical with the figural field emerges in its most systematic form." In fact, de Man defines text within this double perspective as "a generative, open-ended, non-referential grammatical system and as a figural system closed off by a transcendental signification that subverts the grammatical code to which the text owes its existence. The 'definition' of the text also states the impossibility of its existence and prefigures the allegorical narratives of this impossibility."[23]

De Man's type of deconstruction is not the only American type. Christopher Norris sees Geoffrey Hartman as exemplifying much of "what passes for American deconstructionist criticism," which is "an open-ended free play of style and speculative thought, untrammeled by 'rules' of any kind." Norris cites a 1970 essay of Hartman on Milton ("Adam on the Grass with Balsamum") as indication of Hartman's utilization of deconstruction. In the essay, Hartman attempts to overturn the new critics' use of the "problem" of Milton's style to cover their own dislike of his political and religious radicalism. "He defends not only Milton's style but the critic's freedom to adopt a charged and 'answerable' style of his own in order to counter the weight of received opinion. Hartman wants to initiate 'a more adventurous hermeneutic tradition, even at the risk of deepening, provisionally, the difference between criticism and interpretation.'" Hartman is seen as rejecting totally the boundary between literature and theory maintained in the New Criticism. The deconstruction of Hartman (as seen by Norris) is "a deliberate attempt to turn the resources of interpretative style against any too rigid convention of method or language."[24] In chapter 5, Hartman's style of interpretation is illustrated from his use of literary texts to explicate the role of literature in "wording" the "wound" that words have themselves created.

It is possible to see the approach of Hartman as resulting from his experience of the various deconstructions that earlier critics had seen as evolving historically. In such a situation the reader-critic is not primarily interested in drawing out the logic of the text, even if it results in showing how the textual logic is confounded implicitly through the development of

23. Ibid., 270.
24. Norris, *Deconstruction*, 91, 16–17.

figurative tensions. The reader-critic is responding to the text in light of his or her own private struggles. The constructions and deconstructions revolve around the reader. In the case of Hartman, of course, the virtuoso and style in reading do not exist apart from earlier critical evaluations. The role and function of literature in general and of particular literary works for Hartman has been altered by his own experience of literature as well as his place in the history of literary criticism.

Deconstructive criticism, then, may be directed toward the logic involved in reading, and toward relating the text to categories from philosophy and rhetoric. Operating against the background of necessary and inevitable decisions about meaning, deconstruction as carried out by de Man "always has for its target to reveal the existence of hidden articulations and fragmentations within assumedly monadic totalities."[25] But deconstruction may also be oriented in another direction (still against the background of decisions about meaning and the logical uncovering of hidden articulations and fragmentations)—the direction of personal satisfaction and identity. Norris sees critics such as Hartman and Hillis Miller as "happily embracing" the dangers W. K. Wimsatt pointed out in the essay "Battering the Object"—the dangers of dissolving the formal attributes of poetry into the play of interpretative consciousness and of running wild "in games of its own inventing." Norris says that Hartman "makes a virtue and even a vocation of pushing his critical style to the edge of sheer self-indulgence."[26]

From the outside, of course, the readings of Hartman may appear to be exactly as evaluated by Norris. It is possible, however, to see that the readings depend upon the norms and the transformation of norms that have become internalized by the reader-critic. In the process of "play" the reader-critic (consciously or unconsciously) is responding to norms and transformation of norms that are explicitly pointed out by a critic such as de Man. The distinction between the activity of a Hartman and a de Man may simply reflect the distinction between reading and criticism. A reader-critic like Hartman is responding as a reader with theoretical concerns toned down. The critic-reader such as de Man is responding at

25. De Man, *Allegories of Reading*, 249.
26. Norris, *Deconstruction*, 96–97.

a more conscious theoretical level, giving a reading against the background of that critical level.

Values of Deconstruction for Biblical Criticism

The reader-critic who wishes to benefit from deconstructive insights, of course, does not need to opt for one or the other of the paths indicated but may well appropriate insights and practices from both of these as well as other deconstructive modes. What are some of the insights that may be valuable for a biblical reader-critic? One value may be the viewing of biblical texts as literature with "performative" and cognitive dimensions—interdependent dimensions that are intentional in biblical texts. To read a biblical text as literature will mean that attention will be given to "trivial" features and a literary "explanation" will be given to features previously explained by historical or theological arguments. The discoveries resulting from a literary reading will then be seen in relation to earlier (and later) historical and theological readings. The deconstruction of the opposition between the philosophical (or theological or historical) and the literary implies the deconstruction of the opposition between the literal and the metaphorical. As greater importance is accorded to the figurative in the Bible, the figurative may become the norm instead of the exception. In its figurative terms, then, the Bible may be seen as conducting an argument about the literal and figurative.

Deconstruction is suspicious of the notion of theme, and the procedures of deconstruction may be seen as opposed to thematic criticism. Nevertheless, the approach has caused critics to give attention to certain themes or issues in literary works. Just as existentialism has encouraged critics to see what biblical writings as well as avowedly literary works have to say about the relationship between existence and essence, choice, revolt, and the creation of meaning in an absurd universe, deconstruction may sensitize biblical critics to themes or topics such as writing (the relationship between speech and writing), origins, presence and absence, marginality, representation, and indeterminacy.

Deconstruction encourages a style of reading that identifies or produces certain types of structure. Barbara Johnson has described deconstruction as "the careful teasing out of warring forces of signification within the text."[27] From the perspective of "warring forces of signification," Culler suggests the following structures of conflict: the asymmetrical opposition of terms, the condensation and subversion of values in single terms, the text's difference from itself, self-reference, reproduction of conflicts in texts as conflicts between readings of the text, and the subversion of essential elements of the text by marginal elements.[28] These structures of conflict are familiar to biblical students: second terms (which are treated as negative, marginal, or supplementary) turn out to be the condition of possibility of the first; single terms (points of condensation) bring together different values and lines of argument; texts manifest interests that oppose interpretations which the works seem to encourage most emphatically; texts speak obliquely of themselves in descriptions of something else; texts thematize interpretative operations that give life to the tradition of their interpretation in advance; marginal elements in a text call into question and even subvert what are seen as essential elements. Instead of reducing them to historical and theological explanations, a reading informed by deconstructive insights might use the structures of opposition to expand possibilities of meaning.

The deconstruction of the nature of the sign and the distinction between the signifier and the signified means that there are no final meanings that halt the movement of signification. The signified is also in the position of signifier. Readers of biblical texts will continue to look for the signified, but they will respect the characteristic of the signified to become in turn a signifier.

VALIDITY IN INTERPRETATION: E. D. HIRSCH

The work of E. D. Hirsch is not designed to show how a historical reader processes a text from a particular historical vantage point. His purpose is to show that meaning is to be separated from the historical being of the reader. Hirsch's argument for an objective meaning that is related to determinant authorial intention is seen by Lentricchia as "the key" for the traditionalists who oppose linguistic deferral and

27. Barbara Johnson, *The Critical Difference*, 5.
28. Culler, *On Deconstruction*, 213–15.

multivalence.[29] The separation of meaning from the reader must be accomplished if the concept of unchanging textual meaning is to be defended; and Hirsch intends to do just that, to defend the "stable determinacy of meaning."[30]

Valid Interpretation

Author's meaning. In *Validity in Interpretation* (1967), the determinacy of meaning is a result of the author's will because verbal meaning is what the author has willed to convey by a particular sequence of linguistic signs.[31] Validity (not verification or certainty) in interpretation is possible in that it can be shown logically that a given interpretation is more likely to be correct than other interpretations. In the 1967 publication, it is clear that Hirsch's definition of meaning as "what the author meant by his use of a particular sign sequence"[32] is not to be understood in the way that such a statement would normally be construed. Since "an author almost always means more than he is aware of meaning,"[33] room must be made for unconscious meanings and implicit meanings.[34] Nevertheless, these meanings "must lie within the boundary that determines the particular verbal meaning that is being considered."[35] Hirsch uses an iceberg metaphor to relate the different meanings:

> Even though the visible mass is the smaller part, it determines, from the standpoint of anyone examining the iceberg, what belongs to the iceberg as a whole and what does not belong. . . . The self-identity of a verbal meaning depends on a coherence that is at least partly analogous to physical continuity. If a text has traits that point to subconscious meanings (or even conscious ones), these belong to the verbal meaning of the text only if they are coherent with the consciously willed type which defines the meaning as a whole.[36]

The key to validity is the type, the "willed type." Meanings that are coherent with the type belong to verbal meaning. The type is an ideal

29. Lentricchia, *After the New Criticism,* 178.
30. E. D. Hirsch, Jr., *The Aims of Interpretation,* 1.
31. E. D. Hirsch, Jr., *Validity in Interpretation,* 3, 67.
32. Ibid., 8.
33. Ibid., 48.
34. Ibid., 51, 61.
35. Ibid., 51.
36. Ibid., 53–54.

that is able to subsume and represent more than one experience. The idea "tree," for example, can subsume or represent more than one tree or tree experience.[37] The determining characteristics of the type "tree" are common to all trees. To the extent that a person has learned the characteristics of the type, he or she is able to "generate" those characteristics without the characteristics being given. In a 1960 essay, Hirsch had used the concept of *langue* (the language system as opposed to *parole*, the actual concrete act of speaking by an individual) to explicate the "range of meaning possibilities the text can represent. The *langue* of the "speaking subject" is what Hirsch has in mind. This is not to be identified with the "subjectivity of the author as an actual historical person" but is that " 'part' of the author which specifies or determines verbal meaning." The reader must reproduce in him- or herself this *langue*, "the author's 'logic,' his attitudes, his cultural givens, in short his world."[38] A reader may know the type of meaning intended by a speaker through traits such as vocabulary range, syntactical patterns, and formulaic invariants, because the meaning type is grounded in a type of usage.[39]

Interpreter's meaning. In *The Aims of Interpretation*, published in 1976, Hirsch acknowledges that the definition of meaning in the earlier volume was too narrow and normative "in that it restricted meaning to those constructions where the interpreter is governed by his conception of the author's will." The new definition simply states that "meaning is the determinant representation of a text for an interpreter." It is meaning-for-an-interpreter and "comprises constructions where author-ial will is partly or totally disregarded."[40] In fact, already in *Validity in Interpretation*, Hirsch had acknowledged that "there is nothing in the nature of the text itself which requires the reader to set up the author's meaning as his normative idea," even though he argued that "it is preferable to agree that the meaning of a text is the author's meaning" if interpretation is to be conceived of as a corporate enterprise.[41] In *The*

37. Ibid., 265.
38. Ibid., 242–43.
39. Ibid., 80.
40. Hirsch, *Aims*, 79.
41. Hirsch, *Validity*, 24–25.

Aims of Interpretation, Hirsch comes close to those "cognitive atheists" he is opposing by admitting

> the nature of a text is to mean whatever we construe it to mean. . . . We, not our texts, are the makers of the meanings we understand, a text being only an occasion for meaning, in itself an ambiguous form devoid of the consciousness where meaning abides. One meaning of a text can have no higher claim than another on the grounds that it derives from the "nature of interpretation," for all interpreted meanings are ontologically equal; they are all equally real. . . . This ontological equality of all interpreted meaning shows forth in the fact that hermeneutic theory has sanctioned just about every conceivable norm of legitimacy in interpretation. From this historical fact I infer that interpretive norms are not really derived from theory, and that theory codifies *ex post facto* the interpretive norms we already prefer.[42]

The aim of interpretation and the nature of meaning is finally an ethical question in Hirsch's opinion; and he states what he considered to be a "fundamental ethical maxim" for interpretation: "Unless there is a powerful overriding value in disregarding an author's intention (i.e., original meaning), we who interpret as a vocation should not disregard it."[43] Hirsch's concern for an original meaning related to the author's intention, then, can be justified only ex post facto, by concerns beyond textual meaning.

The Role of the Reader

Meaning and significance. Room is provided *logically* by Hirsch for a reader-oriented approach. The type, genre, or frame that serves to guide the reader will inevitably encompass the reader's interests which *may* include the validation of meaning in some objective fashion. In *The Aims of Interpretation,* for example, Hirsch acknowledges that he as well as his opponents are relativists in that "any experience of textual meaning is relative to mind. Objects *for us* are the only objects we have." But he quickly moves away from the implications of such relativism by declaring that the Cartesian subject/object division is still possible by means of the Husserlian bracketing in which the "intentional object" is cleanly separated from the relation of actual human consciousness. The

42. Hirsch, *Aims,* 75–76.
43. Ibid., 90.

term "bracketing" refers to the ability "to demarcate not only a content but also the mental act by which we attend to that content, apart from the rest of our experience." Hirsch uses the expressions "meaning" and "significance" to distinguish the two, and cites ordinary experience as evidence for the ability to differentiate. "The brackets implied by the terms 'meaning' and 'significance' do in fact represent something that most of us believe that we experience in verbal discourse, namely, an alien meaning, something meant by an implied author or speaker who is not ourselves. Whenever we have posited another person's meaning, we have bracketed a region of our experience as being that of another person."[44] At the same time that experience is cited as evidence, Hirsch acknowledges that in practice the separation of meaning and significance is not followed:

> In practice we are always relating our understanding to something else—to ourselves, to our relevant knowledge, to the author's personality, to other, similar works. Usually we cannot even understand a text without perceiving such relationships. . . . Nevertheless, we certainly can isolate or at least emphasize a particular goal for our activity. We can decide at a given moment that we are mainly interested in constructing what the author meant rather than in relating that meaning to something else.[45]

Meaning is even to be distinguished from significance for the author. A difference is to be construed "between what is in a man's verbal meaning and what is outside it, even when that relationship pertains to the author himself or to his subject matter."[46] From the very inception, then, significance accompanies and is inseparable from meaning. Each is defined only in terms of the other. The verbal meaning is ascertained in relation to a significance—for the author as well as for the reader.

The heuristic value of "stable determinacy of meaning." It seems that the expansion of the author's original meaning to include unconscious and implicit meanings consistent with the genre, type, or *langue* of the author (speaking subject) makes the defense of stable determinacy of meaning problematic. Instead of pleading for such a concept on even ethical grounds or opposing such a concept on logical grounds, it is

44. Ibid., 4–6.
45. Hirsch, *Validity*, 140.
46. Ibid., 63.

possible to use the concept of "original meaning" for the hermeneutical prolongation of the text. Indeed, once Hirsch has satisfied himself that he has rescued meaning from cognitive atheists, he delights in the possibility of significance. His distinction between meaning and significance is seen as "a charter of freedom to the critic" because "the liberty of the critic to describe the countless dimensions of a text's significance is closely dependent on his not being constricted by a confusion between significance and meaning."[47]

Parallel to the distinction between meaning and significance, then, is a distinction between interpretation and criticism. Significance (or criticism) is the result of placing meaning into relationship. Hirsch uses the field of biography to illustrate the relationship between criticism and significance. "Interpretation corresponds to the understanding of a man's life as it was lived and experienced, while criticism corresponds to the placing of that life in a larger system of relationships." Significance is limitless, for the verbal meaning of the "shortest and most banal" text can be related to "all conceivable states of affairs—historical, linguistic, psychological, physical, metaphysical, personal, familial, national." It can also be related at different times to "changing conditions in all conceivable states of affairs."[48]

Just as meaning and significance are simultaneous, interpretation (ascertainment of meaning) and criticism (application of meaning) take place simultaneously. The interpreter's mind is in two places at the same time.

When a writer puts on a mask for ironic effect, as in Swift's "A Modest Proposal," the interpreter's mind must be in two places at once as he entertains both the perspective of the modest proposer and the perspective of Swift. In every ironic construction we entertain two perspectives at once, and there is not, I think, any rigid limitation on the number of perspectives we can entertain at once.[49]

In Validity in Interpretation, Hirsch was concerned with establishing criteria for validation of interpretative guesses. He was also concerned that significance be "judicial" and based upon valid interpretation and

47. Ibid., 57.
48. Ibid., 141, 63.
49. Hirsch, Aims, 80.

appropriate in that it always take the purposes of the author into consideration.[50] In *The Aims of Interpretation,* Hirsch comes to the view that the process of validation is in fact a process of arriving at interpretation, that imaginative guesses (hypotheses) and validation accompany one another in the actual establishment of meaning. The process of reading suggested in *Validity in Interpretation* is a twofold process involving an intuitive guess and the critical moment of testing and validation. In *The Aims of Interpretation,* published nearly a decade later, Hirsch sees a closer relationship between understanding and the process of validation. *"The process of understanding is itself a process of validation. . . .* For that which we are understanding is itself an hypothesis constructed by ourselves, a schema, or genre, or type which provokes expectations that are confirmed by our linguistic experience, or when they are not confirmed cause us to adjust our hypothesis or schema."[51] The view of interpretation as "a validating, self-correcting process—an active positing of corrigible schemata which we test and modify in the very process of coming to understand an utterance" is seen by Hirsch as mediating the conflict between the intuitionist (who is "trapped by the fact that communicable language cannot possibly transcend sharable, and therefore public, conventions") and the positivist (who cannot explain how his rules and conventions "can sponsor quite divergent meanings and interpretations"). Hirsch sees features of the phenomena of hypothesis, Edmund Husserl's "intentional object," Jean Piaget's "schema," Wilhelm Dilthey's "whole," and even Martin Heidegger's "preunderstanding" as being "quite identical in their character and function, and also in their connection with what we call meaning."[52]

Once a conventional critic oriented toward historical and original meaning moves as far as Hirsch in the direction of reader's meaning, of what value is the focus on original meaning? It becomes a means instead of an end. It is a construct of the reader that enables the reader to make a sense of the text and by means of the text.

50. Hirsch, *Validity*, 159.
51. Hirsch, *Aims*, 33–34.
52. Ibid., 34–35.

RHETORICAL AND PSYCHOANALYTIC
APPROACHES

The approaches treated in this section—the rhetorical and psychoanalytic approaches represented by Wayne Booth and Norman Holland—must be seen in light of the American new critical heritage and the desire for academically acceptable objectivity. The rhetorical approach that emphasizes the author's imposition of a fictional world upon the reader maintains the autonomy of the text by viewing the reader as a textual reality, with the actual reader carrying out procedures dictated by the author. Psychoanalytic-oriented approaches do not maintain the autonomy of the text, but they establish an objectivity by viewing meaning as the replication of personality or identity in interpretation. Nonetheless, these approaches offer suggestions that can be used in a more radical reader-oriented approach.

The Rhetorical Approach of
Wayne C. Booth

Rhetoric is associated at best (in didactic fiction) with "propaganda" or "instruction." At its worst, it is equated with "crafty calculations." Wayne C. Booth, however, uses the term "rhetoric" positively in his treatment of technique in nondidactic fiction. In *The Rhetoric of Fiction,* he treats the "rhetorical resources available to the writer of epic, novel, or short story as he tries, consciously or unconsciously, to impose his fictional world upon the reader."[53] "Implied" authors and readers constitute a major rhetorical resource for real authors and readers.

The actual reader and the implied author and reader. Booth is not characterizing the speaker in the work ("persona," "mask," or "narrator") as the "implied author"; the speaker in the work is only "one of the elements created by the implied author." The implied author, of course, is also to be distinguished from the real author, for the real author "can seldom afford to pour his untransformed biases into his work." As the author writes, then, he creates "an implied version of 'himself' that is different from the implied authors we meet in other men's works." One

53. Wayne C. Booth, *The Rhetoric of Fiction,* i.

of the most important effects upon the reader is the picture of the presence of this author. "However impersonal he may try to be, his reader will inevitably construct a picture of the official scribe who writes in this manner—and of course that official scribe will never be neutral toward all values. Our reactions to his various commitments, secret or overt, will help to determine our response to the work."[54]

The actual reader's sense of the implied author is built up by numerous elements: "the narrator's explicit commentary," the "kind of tale" the author tells, "the extractable meanings" and the "moral and emotional content of each bit of action and suffering of all of the characters." The sense of the implied author includes, in short, "the intuitive apprehension of a completed artistic whole; the chief value to which *this* implied author is committed, regardless of what party his creator belongs to in real life, is that which is expressed by the total form."[55]

The actual reader is involved in apprehending and building up the picture of the implied author; but in doing this the reader is assuming the role dictated by the author. Alongside the implied author, then, is the implied reader.

> It is only as I read that I become the self whose beliefs must coincide with the author's. Regardless of my real beliefs and practices, I must subordinate my mind and heart to the book if I am to enjoy it to the full. The author creates, in short, an image of himself and another image of his reader; he makes his reader, as he makes his second self, and the most successful reading is the one in which the created selves, author and reader, can find complete agreement.[56]

The implied reader and implied author are constructed in the same process. "Every stroke implying his [the author's] second self will help to mold the reader into the kind of person suited to appreciate such a character and the book he is writing."[57]

The rhetoric by which an author creates the implied reader, then, is the same as that used in creation of the implied author. Most obvious is commentary that is directed outward to the audience (such as that of the chorus in Aeschylus's *Agamemnon* when no other characters are present

54. Ibid., 70–73.
55. Ibid., 73–74.
56. Ibid., 138.
57. Ibid., 89.

and no decisions or actions related to plot are involved). But many of the actual scenes are designed with rhetorical intent. Henrik Ibsen, for example, sometimes "uses such scenes to make the play [*Ghosts*] much more easily intelligible." At other times, "they are used to argue for ideas that the spectator must understand, and at least tentatively entertain, if he is to grasp the play."[58]

Scenes which are really unnecessary to the story (although appropriate to their context) are designed as aids to the reader. Booth defends the integrity of such scenes on the basis of a distinction between the real author and the author's second self. The expanded scene in E. M. Forster's *A Passage to India* in which Dr. Aziz and Mrs. Moore form their initial friendship goes beyond what is necessary for the story.

The real Forster does not need this scene; he knows all this and more about his characters. Only if he imagines himself temporarily as his own reader approaching his work without special knowledge, can we think of him as troubling to write this scene for "himself." Yet, if he postulates himself as reader in this scene, what is he doing that is different from writing with "the reader" in mind? To express this *public* self and to affect a public made up of similar selves become identical processes, and the distinction between expressive and rhetorical theories of literature disappears.[59]

Implied authors and readers as constructs. The conceptualization of Booth is relevant for reader-oriented interpretation whether the text or the reader dominates. The goal of a real reader is to become the implied reader and to find the implied author. It is only in this process that we understand what the literary work really says and does. Booth recognizes (although he does not emphasize) that the real reader must construct the implied author and reader, that the reader constructs the images of the implied author and reader gradually while reading the work. The reading is then validated by the images the reader has constructed. As Susan R. Suleiman suggests, the full recognition of this circularity does not render the notions of implied author and implied reader superfluous, but it does relativize them. "They become no more—and no less—than necessary fictions, guaranteeing the consistency of a specific reading without guaranteeing its validity in any absolute sense."[60]

58. Ibid., 101.
59. Ibid., 109.
60. Suleiman, "Varieties of Audience-Oriented Criticism," 11.

The Psychoanalytic Approach of
Norman N. Holland

The role played in reading and interpretation by individual and personal factors in the lives and experiences of readers has been recognized and then dismissed by many theorists. Those who have studied alterations in the reader brought about by historical change have not considered the psychological factors peculiar to the individual reader a matter of critical concern. Phenomenological approaches recognize the individual element but emphasize the common structural act rather than the individual contribution. Literary scholars in the psychoanalytic tradition, however, have stressed the fact that one cannot know reality apart from one's self and one's own way of knowing. Thus the individuality of the reader or critic is important. The work of Norman N. Holland is used in this section to explicate psychoanalytic-oriented literary criticism and the values it has for reader-oriented theories and methods in general.

The fantasy in the text. In his initial attempts to use psychoanalytic insights in literary criticism, Holland faced the question: "What is the relation between the patterns he finds objectively in the text and a reader's subjective experience of the text?"[61] The basic procedure of a psychoanalytic reading (successive abstraction) was seen by Holland as the New Critical method:

> The skilled reader organizes the details of the text into recurring images and themes. Essentially, he abstracts repeated or contrasted words, images, events, or characters into categories . . . . in *Hamlet*, for example, critics will speak of images of disease, incidents of broken rituals, or characters who do as against characters who talk. . . .
> If a critic wishes to go as far as he possibly can in this process . . . he further reclassifies this first level of abstraction (usually called themes) into a final level consisting of a very few basic terms which the work as a whole is "about." One might, for example, see *Hamlet* as "about" the imperfection that comes between idea and fact. If such a set of terms states the universal intellectual content of the work, if this is its "meaning," then a reader should be able to move from these three very general terms to less general themes like disease, ritual, word-and-deed, and from them back to the text

61. Norman N. Holland, *The Dynamics of Literary Response,* xv.

itself. He should be able to see particular manifestations of one or another of the general terms (imperfections, idea, fact) at any point in the text—or else his generalizations from the text left something out.[62]

Psychoanalysis seeks a central fantasy or daydream which is manifested throughout the text as it has been transformed into social, moral, intellectual, and even mythic terms. Meaning is seen then as a dynamic process of transformation of the unconscious relevance of fantasy into a conscious relevance.

Holland defines fantasies according to customary phases of the child's development, distinguished by the parts of the body or family providing most pleasure or conflict for the child at the time: oral, anal, urethral, phallic, and oedipal. The earliest phase, for example, is the oral phase, the key transaction of which is "self-object differentiation." In literature, the oral phase appears as fantasy related to losing the boundaries of self, being engulfed, overwhelmed, drowned, or devoured (as in Poe's stories of being buried alive).[63]

Literature, however, is not simply a writer's disguised expression of childhood fantasies. Something happens to the fantasies—the same thing that happens in life. "To put the matter very briefly, they get defended against." In literature central nuclear fantasies elude the centering part of our minds by being transformed into meaningfulness. Fantasy thereby achieves an oblique expression and gratification. "In effect, a literary text has implicit in it two dimensions: one reaches 'up' toward the world of social, intellectual, moral and religious concerns; the other reaches 'down' to the dark, chthonic, primitive, bodily part of our mental life."[64]

How does the reader make the implicit upward and downward gropings more or less explicit? Holland suggests that our minds must be split in two as in the process of dreaming. At the same time that we think about the text and supply theme and meaning at the cognitive level, we "introject" the work, feeling the nucleus of the fantasy and the literary treatment of the fantasy as though they were our own.

The theory of "introjected transformation" is summarized by Holland:

62. Ibid., 6–7.
63. Ibid., 35.
64. Ibid., 52, 310.

The literary text provides us with a fantasy which we introject, experiencing it as though it were our own, supplying our own associations to it. The literary work manages this fantasy in two broad ways: by shaping it with formal devices which operate roughly like defenses; by transforming the fantasy toward ego-acceptable meanings—something like sublimation. The pleasure we experience is the feeling of having a fantasy of our own and our own associations to it managed and controlled but at the same time allowed a limited expression and gratification.[65]

The fantasy of the reader. As Holland began to work with the transformational model in teaching, he saw that the response of readers varied far more than could be explained on the basis of a single process "in" the text. In that transition period, Holland was helped by critics such as David Bleich to see the limitations of viewing the literary text as embodiment of the psychological process. "Poems do not fantasize, he [Bleich] pointed out, stories do not have defense mechanisms, and plays do not sublimate—but people do."[66]

The book *Five Readers Reading* grew out of experiments based on the transformational model developed earlier with the additional insight that "psychological processes like fantasies or defenses do not happen in books but people." As the title indicates, the experiences of five readers (given the names Sam, Saul, Shep, Sebastian, and Sandra) formed the basis for the work. The four principles of expectation, defense, fantasy, and transformation are used to describe the interdynamics of the reading experience.

The *principle of expectation* is an overarching principle that incorporates the others: "In general, if a reader has responded positively to a literary work, he has been able to put elements of the work together so they act out his own lifestyle." The reader's lifestyle with which new experiences are approached includes a "characteristic cluster of hopes, desires, fears, and needs." A reader whose hopes are met and who thereby received pleasure will merge with the book and "the events of the book become as real as anything in his mind."[67]

The *principle of defense* declares: "If the reader has a favorable response toward a work, he must have synthesized from it all or part of

---

65. Ibid., 311–12.
66. Norman N. Holland, "A Transactive Account of Transactive Criticism," 181.
67. Norman N. Holland, *Five Readers Reading*, 113–15.

his characteristic structure of defense or adaptation. He must have found something in the work that does what he does to cope with needs or dangers." Defense mechanisms are seen by Holland not as pathological and undesirable blocks to normal pleasure but as "necessary adaptations to inner and outer reality, . . . preconditions without which pleasure would not be possible." The individual's style of defense and adaptation is part of a total lifestyle. Defenses and adaptations in specific contexts are variations of a general pattern or of the individual's "identity theme." This "identity theme" is the broad "central style" that is determined by past events and that forms the foundation for the synthesis of new experiences. This "identity theme" is established in the first stage of a child's development but it grows through experiences (which can be seen as new variations) into an unchanging central theme.[68]

The *principle of fantasy* accompanies the principle of defense as the mode the reader uses to recreate his or her own style through the work.

> Each reader uses the materials he has taken in from the literary work to create a wish-fulfilling fantasy characteristic of himself. The fantasy does not lie latent in the work—only the material for the fantasy that each reader will then create for himself in the terms that give him pleasure (and the fantasy the reader creates may or may not coincide with the fantasy the writer had while writing).[69]

Fantasies are seen by Holland as "clusters of wishes deriving from the stages in which children develop." Readers use materials of the story "to create a fantasy at the level of development" that matters to them.

> No matter how convincing a case I can make for "A Rose for Emily" as a story built on wishes and fears about the control of body products, Sam perceived the story in terms of the masculinity that concerned him, and Saul fantasized about overpowering authorities. Each reader placed the unconscious fantasy content of the story in the level or levels of fantasy where his own mind habitually functioned.[70]

Each of the readers in Holland's experiment "drew on the characters, episodes, and language of what he read" and "structured them into the specific form of fantasy that gave him pleasure, just as he had matched his defenses." Sandra "needed both defensively and libidinally to draw

68. Ibid., 115–16.
69. Ibid., 117.
70. Ibid., 119.

close to sources of strength and nurture," so she tried to fantasize such sources in the stories she read. Saul wanted "to meet the world in a precise bargain" and he "used the materials of the stories to create bargaining situations."[71]

Holland describes the synthesis of the defense structures as "both tricky and subtle" but the use of the story to get the desired fantasy content as "no trouble at all." "The ego's defenses act like a doorkeeper carefully checking invitations against the list of acceptable guests. Once the guests are admitted, however, the party turns out to be not stuffy at all, but quite easygoing, even a bit rowdy and disreputable."[72]

The *principle of transformation* comes into play after the reader has matched defense structures and adapted what has been matched to suit his or her fantasies. The reader

> will "make sense" of the text. By means of such adaptive structures as he has been able to match in the story, he will transform the fantasy content, which he has created from the materials of the story his defenses admitted, into some literary point or theme or interpretation. In doing so, he will use "higher" ego functions, such as his interpretative skills, his literary experience, his experience of human character, in general, his subtlety and sensitivity. He will bring to bear the social, moral, or political ideas that already embody congenial transformations for him. He will, finally, render the fantasy he has synthesized as an intellectual content that is characteristic—and pleasing—for him.[73]

Even though the later work of Holland stresses the "ineffable effect of personality on perception" and the response of readers "in terms of their own 'lifestyle' (or 'character' or 'personality' or 'identity')," the literary text is seen as a constraining reality. The reader is responding to *something*. "The literary text may be only so many marks on a page—at most a matrix of psychological possibilities for its readers. Nevertheless only some possibilities, we would say, truly fit the matrix." The "promptuary" from which the reader builds an experience "includes constraints on how one can put its contents together" even though "these constraints do not coerce anyone."[74]

71. Ibid.
72. Ibid., 121.
73. Ibid., 121–22.
74. Ibid., 4, 8, 12, 286.

Holland sees the text as an "other" over against the reader, and he sees knowledge resulting from the interaction. He speaks, however, not of a "bi-active" model of literary response in which the text causes an "objective" part of the response of the reader and the reader adds a "subjective" variation. He conceives of a literary response as "one indivisible 'transactive' process in which a literent trans-acts—acts across and through—the text to achieve an experience in himself." "In effect, a literent poses questions of the text—the Other—and hears an answer, but always in his own idiolect or in his own personal style of questioning or perceiving or—to introduce a key word—through his identity."[75]

We have spoken about Holland's commitment to "knowledge" and to constraints being set by the text. He admits that a reader is capable of going beyond the constraints set by the writer on "what the reader can or cannot project into the words-on-the-page and how he can or cannot combine them." But if the reader violates the stringencies, "he loses the possibility of sharing his reading with others and winning their support for his lonely and idiosyncratic construct." The necessity of beginning in the experience of sharing with "different subjectivities" is seen as a virtue by Holland in that it allows a consensus about experience "that constitutes all the objectivity subjective beings can have."[76]

The question of the trustworthiness of a method of convergence or consensus is raised by Holland. In answer he contrasts the Cartesian separation of the knower from the known and the view that the knower is "actively synthesizing and re-creating his world from the materials reality provides him." In our situation—"amidst cultural anthropology, the new transactional psychology of perception, Godel's discovery of absolute limits to mathematical axiomatization, the Sapir-Whorf hypothesis in linguistics, and relativity, randomness, and uncertainty even in the 'hard' sciences"—Holland suggests that "it might be possible to say that there is only one way of knowing—the convergence, coherence, or 'fit' of details toward a centering theme or law—but there are different kinds of 'fit.' Which 'fits' are acceptable depends on 'to whom'—the psychology of the researcher."[77]

75. Holland, "A Transactive Account of Transactive Criticism," 181.
76. Holland, *Reading*, 219, 220, 231.
77. Ibid., 279, 280, 281.

The individual and corporate identity and style must not be seen as final determinants in the process of reading and interpretation. These identities are constraints as is the text. There is a "sameness" of literary experience that comes from the "sameness" of the resources used to create these experiences. The differences come from the difference in character. Although the literary work offers constraints for the shaping by the reader, there is a shaping by the reader. The reader "shapes as he perceives, splitting into parts, adding to and omitting from, until his perception matches his particular defensive and adaptive structures." In effect, Holland says, a reader (like Saul or Sebastian) "who has learned to deal with the world in terms of authority must perceive the world as authority before he can deal with it." A person (like Sam or Sandra) "who perceives reality as sources of strength does so because sources of strength match the fears and wishes they experience."[78]

Holland gives an instructive example of how a reader may accommodate the text to his or her own identity even when it appears that the text itself may contain themes that are inconsistent with the reader's identity and resist shaping. Although Sam was "easy going" and able to accommodate to most of the stories read, his "identity" initially prevented a positive response to Hemingway's "The Battler" because of the relationship between Ad and Bugs. He did not like the story because of "critics who tell me that the relationship between Ad and Bugs is essentially homosexual." Holland reports the strategy he used to help Sam respond to the story:

> I felt that throughout our talk about the story, this idea was making him anxious, and toward the end of the interview I gave him an alternative interpretation, that Ad and Bugs are "a pair of rather grotesque and nightmarish parents," Ad supplying the strength and money and Bugs doing the cooking and shopping and nurturing. Sam liked this reading and wondered, "I'm trying to think of why I didn't think of that. . . ." . . .the critical interpretation I offered served him as a way of allaying anxiety. Specifically it said to him that there was a way to nurture and be nurtured without being a homosexual; that he could still keep his boyish masculinity intact; that he could see this in the story and therefore he could be this way himself. The story alone does not yield enough evidence to make me feel I have to choose between the homosexual reading and my familial one. Indeed, I don't think the two readings are really inconsistent. But from Sam's point of view, the familial reading enabled him to deal with a source of

78. Ibid., 247, 225, 226.

anxiety—it enabled him to create a gratifying fantasy from the story through his defensive and adaptive forms, and thus it let the story be a possible source of satisfaction for him.[79]

Is it possible that inconsistency between the identity and style of contemporary readers and that reflected in the biblical texts makes contemporary appropriation problematic? Would the suggestion of Holland be possible for readers of biblical literature or does the nature of biblical literature preclude a creative accommodation of biblical texts to readers' identities? The perception of the nature and function of biblical literature will govern the answer to that question as well as the relevance of many of the insights of reader-oriented literary critics discussed in this chapter.

CONCLUSION

The nature of the reader and the relationship of the reader to linguistic and literary structures and to social and cultural codes are central issues in American literary criticism. The way the question is answered is due in part to the horizon against which it is raised. In American criticism, the horizon of New Criticism is important. Important also is the background of French structuralism and its development in opposition to existentialism. The reader and meaning itself are seen as problematic by some who face the question from such a context. In earlier structural traditions, however, linguistic and literary structures were accommodated to views that saw the reader as an important element in the definition of the literary work of art.

Contemporary deconstruction may be compared with developments in earlier movements in structuralism, movements preceding developments in French structuralism by nearly a half century. Contemporary deconstruction may be seen as a recapitulation of certain stages in the work of scholars such as Sergej Bernstejn, Jurij Tynjanov, and Jan Mukarovsky. An early stage (corresponding to New Criticism and French structuralism) stressed the work of art as a structure of the material aspects of the literary piece. Analysis had the purpose of discovering the organizational features of a work which made it

79. Ibid., 211–12.

aesthetically effective. The organization, however, came to be seen as something not given. Bernstejn emphasized that different points of view can make the same object into different types of literature. Tynjanov saw that different principles of construction are possible for the same work. Mukarovsky began with Tynjanov's concept of the struggle for dominance among components of the work of art and explained the organization of a work on the basis of norms or codes which coexist and intersect in the development of society. A work's organization is only relatively permanent since the aesthetic code responsible for the perception of the work is dynamic.

The difference between Derrida and earlier scholars such as Bernstejn, Tynjanov, and Mukarovsky is that with Derrida and contemporary deconstruction the individual reader is recapitulating the deconstruction and reconstruction which is conceived as taking place over a long period in literary evolution. There is no reigning code or set of codes that authenticate one particular organization. The contemporary reader is capable of decentering and recentering and, hence, observing (and even putting into place) different hierarchies.

The context for decentering or deconstruction in the earlier sense is broader than a particular work. It extends to all of the groupings within which a work may fit and also includes subordinate elements within the work. Tynjanov sees construction not only within an individual work, but within the entire system of literature and between the literary system and other systems. Felix Vodicka emphasized that concretization of an individual work is related to concretizations of the multitude of entities with which that work is related: the "author," genre, literary groups, literary epochs, the literature of a particular nation, and literature as a whole. The concretization (or act of construction) is not accomplished in a strictly scientific way but on the basis of contemporary norms. Again, contemporary deconstruction operates on the basis of the coexistence of different norms and, hence, different constructions at all of the levels. Deconstruction at the level of the total literary system means the undoing of the norms that define the notion of literature itself and the movement of previously "nonliterary" genres, such as philosophical writing, into the literary system. The oppositions serious/nonserious, literal/ metaphorical, and truth/fiction may be taken to distinguish between philosophy and literature (and even after deconstruction we shall continue to understand and appreciate the distinction). The argument of logical positivists that a great deal of what passed for philosophy was not rigorous enough and their attempt to operate within transparent, literal, nonliterary discourse is an example of the assumption of a radical distinction between the seriousness of philosophical discourse and the nonseriousness of literature. Philosophy, however, is always tainted because it cannot escape the linguistic, the literary, and even the rhetorical.

What Derrida says of the task of studying philosophical texts of literature is also true of other types of writings (including biblical texts):

> . . . a task is prescribed: to study the philosophical text in its formal structure, its rhetorical organization, the specificity and diversity of its textual types, its models of exposition and production—beyond what were once called genres—and, further, the space of its stagings and its syntax, which is not just the articulation of its signifieds and its references to being or to truth but also the disposition of its procedures and of everything invested in them. In short, thus to consider philosophy as a "particular literary genre," which draws upon the reserves of a linguistic system, organizing, forcing, or diverting a set of tropological possibilities that are older than philosophy.[80]

This chapter may be read in the context of the two preceding chapters as giving direction to a reader-centered criticism which appreciates the postmodern and deconstructive philosophies and strategies. But at the same time this approach remains committed to an idea of the reader as not merely the plaything of language but someone who is able to make sense in the play of language. The following chapter treats the question of a reader-centered role of literature which will encompass poststructural theories and strategies.

---

80. Jacques Derrida, *Marges de la philosophie*, 348–50. Quoted in Culler, *On Deconstruction*, 181–82.

CHAPTER 5

The Role and Function of Literature

Reader-oriented strategies are helpful for readers and critics who value different levels and sorts of meaning in literary texts. They are able to find a satisfying synthesis in the absence of the possibility of one final meaning. The strategies discussed in this book, of course, are problematic for those who seek the one meaning of a text. Such strategies are even troublesome for those who recognize polyvalence but who attempt to find some synthesis on the basis of older non-reader-oriented concepts of the role and function of literature. Such readers may be overwhelmed with possibilities of meaning and significance because they have no basis for achieving a satisfying synthesis. This chapter attempts to assist in the formulation of a general reader-oriented role or function of literature that may be coordinated with the plethora of reader-oriented strategies. In a radical reader-oriented approach, of course, the particular role will be "concretized" by the reader in the process of reading and interpretation.

THE ROLES OF LITERATURE IN LITERARY CRITICISM

Pleasure or Utility?

Austin Warren suggests that the question of the function of literature is not one instinctively raised by authors and readers. It is when the question is put by "utilitarians and moralists, or by statesmen and philosophers, that is, by the representatives of other special values or the speculative arbiters of all values,"[1] that the poet and reader are forced to make some reasoned response. This does not mean, of course, that there is no function operating to constrain the work of authors and readers. The role or function is so clearly "self-evident" that thought need not be taken of the question. When reasoned response becomes necessary, the assumption of the community as to what functions are possible, and the larger world view governing those assumptions, influence the ways of conceiving of the function of literature—even the conceptualizations of the poets and readers.

The assumptions that were influential in the shaping of Warren's conceptualization of the function of literature centered around the peculiar nature of literature; the "prime and chief function" of literature, therefore, is "fidelity to its own nature." Warren believes that this nature and function is instinctively felt by "proper" and "instinctive" readers as well as by poets. For Warren the "delight" of literature rather than "use" is emphasized. From the Romantic movement on, in the opinion of Warren, the poet has moved away from equating the function of literature with extrinsic relations. When challenged by the community, poets give "the answer which A. C. Bradley calls 'poetry for poetry's sake'. . . ." Nevertheless, Warren sees that the usefulness of literature cannot be denied and that it must be included in a comprehensive view of the function of literature. Pleasure and usefulness coalesce because of the *sort* of pleasure and usefulness involved. "The pleasure of literature . . . is not one preference among a long list of possible pleasures but is a 'higher pleasure' because pleasure in a higher kind of activity, i.e., non-acquisitive contemplation." The utility, on the other hand, does not have to do with duties to be done or lessons to be learned, but with a utility appropriate to non-acquisitive contemplation. The utility of literature, then, is a "pleasurable seriousness," an "aesthetic seriousness," a "seriousness of perception."[2]

In the long history of literary criticism, the utility of literature has not always been subsumed under aesthetic delight. Literature has been seen as conveying knowledge, for example. William K. Wimsatt, Jr., and Cleanth Brooks, indeed, see the history of literary criticism as the

---

1. Austin Warren, "The Function of Literature," 28.
2. Ibid., 28, 21.

progressive attempt to deal with the question of the "kind of knowledge which criticism of a poem, or a poem itself, can lay claim to." They claim that "the entire course of literary theory and criticism, from the time of Plato to the present, has, in effect, been occupied with producing more or less acute versions" of answers to the question "What does a poem say that is worth listening to?"[3]

The perceived nature of the knowledge conveyed by literature has depended upon the context. Aristotle compared literature with history and so literature's knowledge is seen by Aristotle as having to do with the general and the probable. History "relates things which have happened, poetry such as might happen." Warren points out the appropriateness of this judgment when literature is compared with history; but when literature is compared with science, the judgment might be otherwise: "Literature gives a knowledge of those particularities with which science and philosophy are not concerned."[4]

The purpose of literature has also been seen by many as the maintenance of the psyche in a healthy state. The way this function is understood depends upon the reigning psychology. Schiller emphasized the harmonizing of the psyche in terms of eighteenth-century views. I. A. Richards used a form of behaviorism, and F. C. Crews utilized psychoanalytic terms.

Pleasure and Utility

John M. Ellis attempts to mediate the aesthetic delight of literature and the purposefulness of literature in a different fashion than Warren. Each function is proper at its own appropriate level. "The central contrast of this dispute—that between art existing for its own sake on the one hand, and having some useful relation to life on the other, is evidently misconceived. . . ." In attempts to choose between the two apparent alternatives, legitimate functions on the different levels are distorted. "In maintaining that art should not have an overt, direct, purpose 'aesthetes' have failed to think about the function of literature in our lives; it is indeed correct to reject any overt purpose for literature, but an error to think that, because of this, literature has no important

3. William K. Wimsatt, Jr., and Cleanth Brooks, *Literary Criticism*, x.
4. Warren, "Function of Literature," 22.

social function." On the other hand, ". . . the anti-aesthete is right to insist on a social function for literature but quite wrong to deny that the experience of literature is for the reader its own immediate justification; and this error leads him into the even greater error of conceiving the function of literature in terms of overt purpose."[5]

The anti-aesthetic approach to literature may be seen as the cause for the emphasis on the original biographical and historical circumstances of the author. When a literary work is viewed in terms of some overt purpose, it must be assumed the author had that purpose in mind and that such a purpose may be uncovered by historical and biographical study.

Ellis sees functions of literature (not narrow purposes resulting from authors' conscious intentions) being carried out consistent with the aesthetic response. He uses analogies from experiences in life in which we are "impelled by a strong and immediate fascination" that involves "functionally vital actions." Love and play are such experiences. A person "in love" is not thinking primarily of the function of the experience "in terms of the usefulness of a specific pair-bond in the human pattern of child-rearing." Love is a powerful experience with its own justification. The child at play is not thinking of "the gradual exercising of the child's capacities before it becomes mature and must exercise them in 'real' situations." To children, play is its own value. Yet love and play have important functions, more important, it seems, than if the experience involved directly purposeful behavior. "Important functions are reinforced by enjoyment of the behavior fulfilling those functions."[6]

The functioning of literature in the sense accepted by Ellis is an empirical matter related to social structures as well as to the structures of the literary texts. One outstanding function may grow out of the unusual social situation in which people live:

> Man lives in social units composed of large numbers of his fellows, and yet remains an ingenious, opportunistic, aggressive individual, quite unlike the typical herd animal in nature. His behavior is in many ways like that of more solitary territorial animals, who do not get on well with their fellows. And yet, he must live in a large, precarious, and unstable social unit.[7]

5. John M. Ellis, *The Theory of Literary Criticism*, 240.
6. Ibid., 238–39.
7. Ibid., 244.

In typical social situations, there is no scope for the exercise of all of the individual's capacities. It would be dangerous for all of society if individuals lived the life of daily danger and opportunity for which humans are genetically fitted. On the other hand, it is also dangerous to have human capacities too much out of step with actual life.

Perhaps, then, one of the outstanding functions of literature is to deal with this situation; it can offer us dramatic and violent experiences without the actual drama and violence that would threaten the stability of our society, and in more general terms can increase the content of our experience to compensate for the reduction it must suffer if we are to live together in such potentially dangerous groups.[8]

Another function is the assistance literature gives in the creation of a "sense of the cohesion of a social unit the extent of which is invisible to the individual." The transmission of social values is involved in this creation of a sense of cohesion, and is often cited as an educational function. Ellis, however, sees a more important function of literature in education as "the development of the important power of the imagination."[9] The function of literature is seen by Ellis as dynamic. Differences exist because of differences in social structures. Nevertheless, utility is implicit in the nature of literature even if the specific utilization depends upon the particular society within which the literature functions.

Pleasure and Utility from the Reader's Perspective

It is instructive to reconceptualize the relationship of the two poles of literary experience, pleasure and usefulness, from a reader-oriented rather than a social perspective. Some of the specific functions noted by Ellis are related to the individual reader as much as to society—accommodation to social constraints and development of the imagination, for example. Moreover, the passive society may be reconceptualized as the active "readership." Warren reaches toward this dynamic reader-oriented perspective in his attempt to adjudicate between the different views of the "cathartic" function of literature. Does literature relieve us of emotions by allowing us to express them or does it rather excite

8. Ibid.
9. Ibid., 245.

emotions? Warren asks if there is a difference in literature itself or "are we to distinguish between groups of readers and the nature of their response?" Warren's assumption about the nature of literature turns him away from the reader-oriented view to the conclusion that for "proper readers" literature does not excite emotions. The emotions represented in literature are "recollected in tranquillity" by such readers. They are "the *feelings* of emotions."[10]

The failure to include the reader in the ontological definition of the literary work of art accounts for Warren's failure to take seriously the suggestion that different but legitimate functions coexist among different readers. When the role of the reader is seen as a necessary ingredient in the definition of a literary work of art, the conception of the nature of the work and its function is transformed.

The "reader" in the contemporary situation is not the autonomous subject of Descartes. The death of the idea of some static foundation for world and humankind has resulted in the death of the idea of a static autonomous self. The contemporary reader is not defined apart from world, apart from "play" in various fields, including the significant field of language. Humankind is not the governor in the play of language, but humans are involved. James S. Hans provides a perspective on contemporary concepts of human being and language that helps us see a contemporary role for literature.

> Language may be an instrument, but only in the same sense that feet are instruments: our language takes us where we want to go, but we often don't know precisely where we want to go, so, given a general direction, we follow the play of language that is inaugurated by our orientation. That it takes us down paths we hadn't originally foreseen is important, but so is the fact that we have provided the general direction ourselves. . . . Language is always used for specific purposes in one sense, but it is used most productively when the specific purposes give way to the play within the field of language, when the play itself takes over and places our specific purposes into the larger perspective of its own play.[11]

Contemporary critics have attempted to restate the function of literature in light of a new conceptualization of the nature of the reader and of the literary work of art.

10. Warren, "Function of Literature," 28.
11. James S. Hans, *The Play of the World*, 105.

Georges Poulet. Poulet emphasizes the achievement of self-transcendence through the self-effacement of the reading process. In reading, a reader replaces surrounding physical objects with mental objects, a universe infinitely more elastic than the world of physical objects. The object of the reader's thought is the thoughts of another, yet it is the reader who is their subject in the act of reading. "I feel sure that as soon as I think something, that something becomes in some indefinable way my own. Whatever I think is a part of *my* mental world. And yet here I am thinking a thought which manifestly belongs to another mental world, which is being thought in me just as though I did not exist."[12]

In reading that involves the total commitment of the reader, the subject exists in the work. And in the moment of reading "what matters to me is to live, from the inside, in a certain identity with the work and with the work alone. . . . Nothing external to the work could possibly share the extraordinary claim which the work now exerts on me."[13]

The conventional linguistic and literary structures, the activities of readers actualizing the literary work, and the meanings ordinarily found in literary works are not denied. All these are subordinated, however. Beyond the "subjective activity present in a literary work" that may be partially "explained by its relationship with forms and objects within the work" there exists "a subject which reveals itself to itself (and to me) in its transcendence relative to all which is reflected in it." From this perspective, Poulet suggests that criticism must move beyond the objective elements of the work (to "annihilate" or at least "momentarily to forget" these elements) with the purpose of elevating itself "to the apprehension of a subjectivity without objectivity."[14]

Stanley E. Fish. Fish redefines literature and meaning because of his view of the significance of the reader's responses. Literature, in his opinion, is a kinetic art, an art "which refuses to stay still." This view of literature opposes the objectivity of the text: "The objectivity of the text is an illusion, and moreover, a dangerous illusion, because it is so physically convincing. The illusion is one of self-sufficiency and

12. Georges Poulet, "Criticism and the Experience of Interiority," 44.
13. Ibid., 46.
14. Ibid., 48–49.

completeness." The ready availability of the book, its presence on the shelf, and its listing in the library's catalogue encourage us to think of the book as a stationary object. Although we do not *experience* a stationary object, when we put the book back after reading we forget that *"it* was moving . . . and *we* were moving with it" as we read.[15]

A criticism that sees the literary work itself as an object for critical judgment

> extends this forgetting into a principle; it transforms a temporal experience into a spatial one; it steps back and in a single glance takes in a whole (sentence, page, work) which the reader knows (if at all) only bit by bit, moment by moment. It is a criticism that takes as its (self-restricted) area the physical dimensions of the artifact and within these dimensions it marks out beginnings, middles, and ends, discovers frequency distributions, traces out patterns of imagery, diagrams strata of complexity (vertical of course), all without ever taking into account the relationship (if any) between its data and their affective force. Its question is what goes into the work rather than what does the work go into.[16]

Fish declares that the merit of kinetic art is that it "forces you to be aware of 'it' as a changing object—and therefore no 'object' at all—and also to be aware of yourself as correspondingly changing." Since meaning for Fish is an experience the reader has in the course of reading, he is not really concerned for the discovery of new areas of the self or the development of the self in broad terms. He describes his method as "an analysis of the developing responses of the reader to the words as they succeed one another on the page." Fish suggests that the word "meaning" conveys the notion of message or point and should perhaps be discarded since "the meaning of an utterance . . . is its experience—all of it—and that experience is immediately compromised the moment you say anything about it."[17]

Wolfgang Iser. Iser emphasizes the reader's use of imagination in the concretization of texts and sees the process as pleasurable and leading to a fuller knowledge of the self and even to self-creation. The creative activity of the reader in the act of reading results in the "virtual

15. Stanley E. Fish, "Literature in the Reader," 82–83.
16. Ibid., 83.
17. Ibid., 83, 85, 98.

dimension of the text" and endows the text with reality. The coming together of text and imagination transforms the text into an experience for the reader. This experience takes place through a "process of continual modification" that is "closely akin to the way in which we gather experience in life." Because of the nature of this process, the "reality" of the experience of reading illuminates the basic patterns of real experience. As a "living event" the experience of reading obliges the reader to seek continually for consistency which allows her or him to "close up situations and comprehend the unfamiliar." In the process of consistency building, the reader is constantly forced to make decisions that both include and exclude possibilities. What is excluded, however, becomes a reality that takes effect as a "latent disturbance of the consistency established." Iser indicates that the reader is thus entangled in the text *Gestalt* produced.

> Through this entanglement the reader is bound to open himself up to the workings of the text and so leave behind his own preconceptions. . . . Reading reflects the structure of experience to the extent that we must suspend the ideas and attitudes that shape our own personality before we can experience the unfamiliar world of literary texts. But during this process, something happens to us.[18]

Iser sees the same process as Poulet (the convergence of text and reader), but Iser attributes this not to the invasion of one's consciousness by the consciousness of another but to an artificial division of one's personality.

> Although we may be thinking the thoughts of someone else, what we are will not disappear completely—it will merely remain a more or less powerful virtual force. . . . Every text we read draws a different boundary within our personality, so that the virtual background (the real "me") will take on a different form, according to the theme of the text concerned. This is inevitable, if only for the fact that the relationship between alien theme and virtual background is what makes it possible for the unfamiliar to be understood.[19]

The act of reading, in Iser's conceptualization, does involve being in a position to conceive and understand something we have not experienced.

18. Wolfgang Iser, "The Reading Process," 65.
19. Ibid., 67.

But "such acts of conception are possible and successful to the degree that they lead to something being formulated in us." The formulation of the unformulated in the reading process, then, extends to the formulation of ourselves.[20]

Jonathan Culler. In *Structuralist Poetics* Culler emphasized a mode of interpretation based on literary creation itself. He does not see this as replacing thematic interpretation or as denying statements about world; and he does not deny that literary works can be enjoyed for reasons that are essentially unrelated to his concept of understanding of "literary competence." Nevertheless, Culler emphasizes the conventions of poetry, the logic of symbols, and the operations for production of poetic effects as the basis of literary forms that can be studied as operations performed by readers. This is a "reversal of critical perspective" in that it grants precedence to the task of formulating a theory of literary competence and it relegates critical interpretation to a secondary role. What may be thought of as "facts about various literary texts" are reformulated as "conventions of literature and operations of reading."[21]

Culler sees humane values in the "revitalizing powers of a structuralist poetics." The making explicit of what one does when reading or interpreting a literary text results in considerable gain "in self-awareness and awareness of the nature of literature as an institution." When one assumes that what one is doing is natural, it is difficult to gain an understanding of what is being done. When reading is seen as an activity that is not innocent but charged with artifice, however, one sees that literature is different from other modes of discourse about the world. "These differences lie in the work of the literary sign: in the ways in which meaning is produced." The acceptance of Culler's view of literature as "an institution composed of a variety of interpretive operations" leads to "that questioning of the self and of ordinary social modes of understanding which has always been the result of the greatest literature." Literature then "challenges the limits we set to the self as a device or order and allows us, painfully or joyfully, to accede to an expansion of self." In the mode of interpretation based on poetics itself,

---

20. Ibid.
21. Jonathan Culler, "Literary Competence," 115.

"one's interpretation is an account of the ways in which the work complies with or undermines our procedures for making sense of things. . . . In this kind of interpretation the meaning of the work is what it shows the reader, by the acrobatics in which it involves him, about the problems of his condition as *homo significans,* maker and reader of signs."[22]

Paul Hernadi. Hernadi would combine the various possibilities of use and delight of literature by the conceptualization of literary texts as "things said" and "things made." The text is normally regarded as a "thing said." We see the text as "a sequence of words through which a writer or speaker, using a particular system of verbal signs, conveys some information to readers or listeners." As a "thing said" a text communicates between the writer or speaker and the reader or listener and also represents or "connects" a verbal sequence with what it conceptually signifies and evokes. Two types of concerns result from the consideration of the text as a "thing said." One is "the ethical concern with the *correspondence* between the actual writer's or speaker's intentions and the likely impact of his text or utterance on actual readers or listeners." The other concern is the "cognitive concern with the *correspondence* between the information conveyed by a contemplated sequence of words and particular details of our own view of the representable world."[23]

But the text is also a "thing made" for benefit and pleasure. Horace's advice to combine the useful and the sweet was given "to facilitate simultaneous success with both the older and younger members of the poet's audience." The young and old in the individual human psyche are also appealed to simultaneously by literature. "The 'young' wants to be entertained through thrill and gratification, while 'the old' wants to be committed within cosmic (natural or supernatural) and social contexts." Hernadi indicates that in his view "the most representative 'things made' . . . will help to achieve a delicate balance between the self-assertive need for pleasurable entertainment and the self-transcending need for beneficial commitment in each of us." It is especially when "presumably non-aesthetic values of a literary work" are released centrifugally from

22. Ibid., 116-17.
23. Paul Hernadi, "Introduction," *What Is Literature?* xviii–xix.

the "direct contact" with corresponding life values that these values "turn out to be promoting the dynamic equilibrium of such quasi-aesthetic attitudes as the (tragic) endurance of the painfully finite, the (comic) indulgence in the desirably varied, the (satirical) indignation over the curably incongruent, and the (romantic) admiration for the awe-inspiring sublime aspects of the human condition."[24]

As "things said" (or as vehicles of communication and representation) literary works "tend to balance as much expressive intensity, persuasive power, verbal design, and informational coherence as can mutually enhance each other." As "things made" (occasions for entertainment and commitment), literary works are "geared to promote the humanizing mediation between the extremes of self-sufficiency and self-transcendence: the coarser varieties of thrill or gratification on the one hand, the more radical versions of cosmic or social disparagement of individual life on the other."[25]

Geoffrey Hartman. In the concluding chapter of *Saving the Text*, Hartman proposes a counterstatement to Derrida that constitutes a role for literary study in the deconstructionist mode: "to word a wound words have made." Antirepresentational modes of questioning deconstruct the illusion that particular texts "have a direct, even original, relation to what they represent." What seems to be a cause (reality, presence) is in fact an effect, an illusion of depth. Hartman, however, sees that there is a "reality of the effect" that is inseparable from the "reality of words." He feels that the movement of liberation of language from representational concepts "should not cheapen the mimetic and affectional power of words, their interpersonal impact." The subject of the final chapter of *Saving the Text* is the reality of the effect "in its discernible, empirical nearness, in its moral and mimetic impact."[26]

The wounding that results from the equivocal nature of words and the lack of satisfaction of demands of the psyche grows out of the "expectation that a self can be defined or constituted by words, if they are direct enough, and the traumatic consequences of that expectation."

24. Ibid., xix–xxi.
25. Ibid., xxi.
26. Geoffrey Hartman, *Saving the Text*, 121, 120.

But literature has a "medicinal function" which is "to word a wound words have made." Words themselves help us tolerate the normal condition of "partial knowledge" that is the condition of living in the context of words. Hartman explains the fact that "literature sweats balm, and heals the wound words help to produce" by an emphasis on the relationship of the recognitive function of language.

> To put the entire emphasis on the cognitive function . . . will damage the recognitive function . . . and the language exchange as a whole. Values continue to be created that may seem purely ritual, or not entirely perspicuous. Even when art represents a movement from ignorance to knowledge, it is not for the sake of clearing up a simple misunderstanding or emending the human mind in an absolute manner.[27]

In his conclusion to "Words and Wounds," Hartman comes close to explaining what he has described earlier in literary terms—the affective volitional closure and its relation to cognition. He quotes Stanley Cavell to the effect that empirical statements are statements that claim truth and depend upon evidence while truthful statements are statements that claim truthfulness and depend upon our acceptance of them. A true statement is something we know or do not know; a truthful statement, on the other hand, is one we acknowledge or fail to acknowledge. Acknowledgment is the "recognition" that is beyond cognition and that brings closure and the healing of the wounded spirit. But the truth that depends upon evidence and the truthfulness that involves acknowledgment or recognition cannot be divorced. Hartman admits that the very desire manifested in his essay is an "aesthetic" maneuver to master the "intolerable ear-fear" by converting it into the will "to establish the ideal of science as pure cognition or disinterested knowledge." Knowledge desired in the form of *theoria* or *imitatio* is also pleasurable. The quietus sought in logic subverts logic itself.[28]

Hartman denies that we can get beyond words. Words (threatening by their nature) must be heeded. But they need not be taken literally; life need not be lived under their sway. The closure of figurative action substitutes another meaning for the dread words, but this action constitutes "another set of words."

27. Ibid., 131, 133, 134, 137.
28. Ibid., 157.

> Words have been found that close the path to the original words. This absolute closure is what we respond to, this appearance of definitive detachment and substitution. The words themselves block the way. There is no going back, no stumbling through ghostly or psychoanalytic vaults: the "dread voice" exists as the poem or not at all.[29]

The Reader as Subject and as Object of Language. Reader-oriented views of the role and function of literature define the role vis-à-vis the reader. The ultimate significance is for the reader and the other aspects of literature are subordinated to or at least coordinated with reader-significance. The relationship between reader as subject (acting upon the text) and reader as object (being acted upon by the text), however, is not seen as an opposition but as two sides of the same coin. It is only as the reader is subject of text and language that the reader becomes object. It is as the reader becomes object that the fullness of the reader's needs and desires as subject are met.

After a lengthy history of trying to subjugate the world by means of language and of trying to subjugate language itself, says Hans, "we have arrived at the point where we should be capable of listening to language and allowing ourselves to be played by it." This is a new concept of the role of the individual human being, indeed a new concept of humankind. Hans accepts the expression "the end of man" as a legitimate way of speaking of the role of readers in our current situation. To speak of "the end of man," however,

> is not to deny the human or to act as if it doesn't exist; it is simply a way to reenregister our views of the activities in which we participate in a way which places the human in a more modest, though still important, place. Our location is never central because there never is a central location; . . . . In this sense, the end of man means simply the beginning of a different kind of human, that moment in which we first take up our location and understand its potentialities and limitation in order to begin to take upon ourselves the play of production to which we rightfully belong.[30]

The play of language is inaugurated by the orientation of readers. That language "takes us down paths we hadn't originally foreseen," is true, but true also is the fact that "we have provided the general direction ourselves." When the play of language takes over, it "places our specific

---

29. Ibid.
30. Hans, *Play of the World*, 198–99.

purposes into the larger perspective of its own play." This play of language, then, "is one of the chief ways through which we confirm or deny the value of specific propositions for which we are using language at any particular time." The situation is simple but profound: the reader's instrumental approach to language allows the play within the field of language. This play of language then doubles back to the instrumental use. In this process language "generates the conventions of perception and orientation by which we order our lives," but "it also constantly changes those conventions through play with other fields. . . ." This is possible because the reader does not remain within the endless play of language but relates the play of language to the play of other fields. This more comprehensive play is one "that is activated by the orientation man applies, through language, to the situations that confront him."[31]

The role of literature in the life of the reader is to be seen as related to knowledge that the text makes possible for the reader—knowledge extending beyond the world of the text to the world uncovered by the text. It is to be seen in light of cognitive and noncognitive affective experiences of the reader in the process of making sense of the text as knowledge. It is to be seen in the light of the development of self-knowledge vis-à-vis the world of the text and the process of reading. Is it possible to conceptualize an overarching role that does justice to the interrelated functions? Lotman suggests that literature aims at "a knowledge of the world and the relationships among people, self-knowledge, and the development of the human personality in the process of learning and social communication. In the final summing up, the goal of poetry coincides with the goal of culture as a whole."[32] Literature with all of its meanings and meaning-effects may be seen as the instrument for humankind discovering, creating, and/or making sense of world, self, and whatever world-and-self-transcending meanings and values humankind is capable of imaging. The specific role of a particular text (or group of texts) may be seen in light of development of self and human personality, with the achievement of cognitive knowledge being a penultimate function. The role, however, may be perceived more in light of knowledge of the world to be achieved by the

31. Ibid., 105.
32. Jurij Lotman, *Analysis of the Poetic Text*, 132.

reader, the effect of such knowledge and its achievement on the reader and the reader's world being toned down but not eliminated.

INTERPRETATION AND VALIDATION

Interpretation

The reader's role in the reader-centered concept of literature's function is to enter into a transactive relationship with the text through analysis and synthesis, by means of the codes and rules, conventions and strategies that the reader finds compelling and satisfying. One controlling strategy in the process is interpretation. Interpretation is the translation or recording of aspects of meaning uncovered and experienced by the reader into some sort of language and conceptuality shared by a community of contemporaries. The statements of meaning will be constrained by the community and its critical methods as well as by the text and the reader's capacity and experience in reading and interpretation. The methodological reduction of a text to the various historical perspectives, to existential categories, to contemporary sociological theory, and to other codes, therefore, is legitimate in a reader-centered approach. The interpretive language and conceptuality, however, will not be seen as capable of containing all of the potential meanings or even all of the meanings possible in terms of the given language (history, philosophy, sociology, ethics, theology, psychology, etc.). This is the difference between a positivistic approach and a reader-oriented approach. No one code or system is able to exhaust the potentialities of the text. This awareness relativizes the interpretation resulting from the application of any one code or set of codes.

Those readers and critics who are interested in synthesis of the meanings from various levels, fields, and epochs will emphasize continuity among the different meanings, but this will not result in a completely final synthesis. In the readers' transformation of Paul's Letter to the Galatians into a literary work, for instance, serious attention is given to the linguistic and literary material itself; it is not seen as the dispensable container of an original message. The message, moreover, is generalized. It is no longer directed simply to a first-century congregation in the Roman province of Galatia but to all individuals and groups who face the conflict between external constraint and the vocation of freedom. Attention to the writing as a "letter" and to its rhetorical organization and devices will be coordinated with the "message" to its original readers and to its expanding audience. The world of ideas and values that make such a vision possible will be imaged by perceptive readers; such a world will become the backdrop for evaluating statements of the letter and normative statements that can be made on the basis of the letter. Perhaps the reader will question the nature of some of the statements of the author (attacks upon opponents, for example) in light of the world of values that supports the positive affirmations. The less-positive statements may then be seen not simply as limitations in the historical author but as literary and rhetorical devices.

In spite of the possibility of seeing continuity between meanings of different levels, fields, and epochs, there are discontinuities. Interpretation as a final synthesis eludes us. Because of the impossibility of a final statement of meaning (and because the statement of meaning may be less significant than the process of achieving meaning), the idea of interpretation has been found questionable. Is it not possible to value the partiality of interpretation positively? Is truth or truthfulness in interpretation necessarily ruled out? It is possible, in fact, to reevaluate the relativism of methods and meanings not to say that truth is unattainable but that truth is attainable in all of the various locations and universes of humankind. Truth is discovered and expressed in terms that make sense within a particular universe of meaning. It is not some final objective transhistorical and transhuman expression of truth, for truth in such a form does not touch us. But meanings that are consistent with the various systems that cohere in a particular universe of meaning are true—or truthful. The universe, of course, includes us, the inhabitants of that universe who use such truth in making sense for ourselves, but it also includes elements over against us that are involved in our making sense of world and self.

Validation

The criteria for validation of reading and interpretation are transformed in a reader-oriented approach. The actual forces that operate to enable and constrain the reading and interpretation are the same for validation: the reader (or readership) *makes* a sense in light of a particular "set," within a particular cultural setting, by means of codes supplied and validated by that culture. The reader is the touchstone for meaning and validation. When a reader says that the text means thus-and-so for her or him, that fact cannot be challenged (assuming the truthfulness of the reader). That is, the reader has come to a satisfying synthesis on the basis of the various textual and extratextual factors that play a part in reading and interpretation. Other readers are not obliged to agree; therefore, the interpreter has to persuade others that the synthesis is in accord with the various factors. Other readers, meanwhile, are able to show that there is a lack of accord or that factors ignored by the interpreter make another synthesis preferable. The validity of interpretation—as it moves from the individual to the community—is intersubjective. An interpretation is valid when a group of readers and interpreters agree that it is valid.

On what basis can such agreement be secured? On the basis of the "fit" between the interpretation and the various textual and extratextual factors. This "fit" is itself not a completely objective criterion. An interpreter or a group of interpreters may favor one factor over another or ignore factors important to other interpreters. Some contemporary reader-oriented interpreters emphasize the significance for the contemporary reader to such an extent that the need for faithfulness to some original purpose and meaning is negligible. The broad role and function of the text as literature takes precedence over the narrow original purpose. Augustine took that position in his approach to biblical interpretation. He distinguished between use and enjoyment. "To use . . . is to employ whatever means are at one's disposal to obtain what one desires." To enjoy a thing is to "rest with satisfaction in it for its own sake." The end of biblical literature, for Augustine, is love of God and neighbor, the "love of an object which is to be enjoyed, and the love of an object which can enjoy that other in fellowship with ourselves." This goal may be achieved even when the meaning drawn from the text is not "the precise meaning which the author . . . intends to express in that place." If a mistake in interpretation tends to build up love, in Augustine's opinion, the interpreter "goes astray in much the same way as a man who by mistake quits the high road, but yet reaches through the fields the same place to which the road leads."[33]

33. Augustine, *On Christian Doctrine*, Book I, iv, 4; v, 5; xxxv, 39; xxxvi, 40.

E. D. Hirsch may not be far from that position in his conclusion that validation is not in terms of some narrow original intention of an author, but in terms of the genre, type, or *langue*. When an interpretation is faithful to the *sort* of meaning intended, the interpretation is valid even if it is a meaning not in the mind of the original author. A reader-centered approach *may* give more attention to the objective criteria for the type or genre noted by earlier interpreters, but the reader may eventually transcend those externally imposed criteria and become equal to the type. Hirsch, beginning from the objective side, says the reader must reproduce in himself the "logic" of the author, the *langue*, in short the "world" of the author, in order to make sense which is valid. Beginning from the other pole, emphasis would be made upon the actualization of the *langue* by the reader, or at least the coalescence of the sort of meaning intended by the author and the sort of meaning intended by the reader.

CONCLUSION

Readers make sense. Conviction that there is meaning precedes the discovery and creation of meaning. Readers have made sense of the Bible as words and the Word, as human action and divine event, as an object of critical scrutiny and as the subject of human salvation and freedom. The sort of meaning sought has constrained the method used and the meaning found. A thesis of this book has been that reader-meaning has accompanied even the most radically objective historical approach. The reader is the touchstone for the sort of meaning desired, the method, the validity of the result.

This does not mean that "anything goes," for systems of interpretation involve components that must be correlated with each other and with the reader—components that are dynamic in themselves as well as parts of a dynamic system. These components include a world view that constrains the sort of meaning desirable and possible, methods that are capable of discerning those sorts of meaning, and meanings and interpretations that are consistent with the world view and the methods employed and which satisfy the reader.

The method is not static—it is dynamic and capable of accommodating itself to whatever world view directs our living and thinking. It is

Works Cited

Abrams, M. H. *The Mirror and the Lamp: Romantic Theory and the Critical Tradition.* New York: W. W. Norton, 1958.

Adams, Marilyn Jager, and Allan Collins. "A Schema-Theoretic View of Reading." In *New Directions in Discourse Processing,* ed. Roy O. Freedle, 1–22. Norwood, N.J.: Ablex Publishing, 1979.

Aristotle, *The Poetics.* In *On Poetry and Style,* trans. G. M. A. Grube, 3–62. Indianapolis and New York: Bobbs-Merrill, 1958.

———. *On Poetry and Style.* Trans. with an introduction by G. M. A. Grube. Indianapolis and New York: Bobbs-Merrill, 1958.

Augustine. *On Christian Doctrine.* In *A Select Library of the Nicene and Post-Nicene Fathers of the Christian Church,* 2:513–619. Ed. Philip Schaff. New York: Charles Scribner's Sons, 1903.

Barthes, Roland. *S/Z.* Eng. trans. Richard Miller. London: Jonathan Cape, 1975.

Bernstejn, Sergej. "Ästhetische Voraussetzungen einer Theorie der Deklamation." In *Texte der Russischen Formalisten,* 2:338–85. Munich: Wilhelm Fink, 1972.

Booth, Wayne C. *The Rhetoric of Fiction.* Chicago and London: University of Chicago Press, 1961.

Bremond, Claude. "Morphology of the French Folktale." *Semiotica* 2 (1970): 247–76.

Crane, R. S. *The Idea of the Humanities and Other Essays: Critical and Historical.* Chicago and London: University of Chicago Press, 1967.

Culler, Jonathan. "Defining Narrative Units." In *Style and Structure in Literature,* ed. Roger Fowler, 123–42. Ithaca, N.Y.: Cornell University Press, 1975.

———. "Literary Competence." In *Reader-Response Criticism: From Formalism to Post-Structuralism,* ed. Jane P. Tompkins, 101–17. Baltimore and London: Johns Hopkins University Press, 1980. Reprinted from

135

Jonathan Culler, *Structuralist Poetics*, 113–30. London: Routledge & Kegan Paul, 1975.

_____. "Making Sense." *Twentieth Century Studies* (December 1974): 27-36.

_____. *On Deconstruction: Theory and Criticism after Structuralism*. London, Melbourne, and Henley: Routledge & Kegan Paul, 1983.

De Man, Paul. *Allegories of Reading: Figural Language in Rousseau, Nietzsche, Rilke, and Proust*. New Haven, Conn.: Yale University Press, 1979.

Derrida, Jacques. *Limited Inc*. Eng. trans. in *Glyph* 2 (1977): 162–254.

_____. "Living On." In *Deconstruction and Criticism*, ed. Geoffrey H. Hartman, 75–176. New York: Seabury Press, 1979.

_____. *Marges de la philosophie*. Paris: Minuit, 1972.

_____. *Of Grammatology*. Eng. trans. Gayatri Chakrovorty Spivak. Baltimore: Johns Hopkins Press, 1976.

_____. "Structure, Sign, and Play in the Discourse of the Human Sciences." In *The Languages of Criticism and the Sciences of Man: The Structuralist Controversy*, ed. Richard Macksey and Eugenio Donato, 247–65. Baltimore and London: Johns Hopkins Press, 1972.

Dodd, C. H. *The Parables of the Kingdom*. New York: Charles Scribner's Sons, 1961.

Dundes, Alan R. *The Morphology of North American Indian Folktales*. Folklore Fellows Communications no. 195. Helsinki: Suomalainen Tiedeakatemia, 1964.

Ellis, John M. *The Theory of Literary Criticism: A Logical Analysis*. Berkeley, Los Angeles, and London: University of California Press, 1974.

Fish, Stanley E. "Literature in the Reader: Affective Stylistics." In *Reader-Response Criticism: From Formalism to Post-Structuralism*, ed. Jane P. Tompkins, 70–100. Baltimore and London: Johns Hopkins University Press, 1980. Reprinted as the appendix to *Self-Consuming Artifacts*. Berkeley and Los Angeles: University of California Press, 1972.

Fokkema, D. W., and Elrud Kunne-Ibsch. *Theories of Literature in the Twentieth Century: Structuralism, Marxism, Aesthetics of Reception, Semiotics*. London: C. Hurst, 1977.

Foucault, Michel. *The Archaeology of Knowledge*. Eng. trans. A. M. Sheridan Smith. New York: Harper & Row, 1976.

Freedle, Roy O., ed. *New Directions in Discourse Processing*. Advances in Discourse Processes, vol. 2. Norwood, N.J.: Ablex Publishing, 1979.

Frye, Northrop. *The Great Code: The Bible and Literature*. San Diego, New York, and London: Harcourt Brace Jovanovich, 1982.

Greimas, A. J., and F. Rastier. "The Interaction of Semiotic Constraints." *Yale French Studies* 41 (1968): 86–105.

Güttgemanns, Erhardt. "Narrative Analyse synoptischer Texte." *Linguistica Biblica* 25/26 (1973): 50–73.

Hans, James S. *The Play of the World*. Amherst: University of Massachusetts Press, 1981.

Hartman, Geoffrey H. "Literary Criticism and Its Discontents." *Critical Inquiry* 3 (1976).

_____. *Saving the Text: Literature/Derrida/Philosophy*. Baltimore and London: Johns Hopkins University Press, 1981.

Hernadi, Paul, ed. *What Is Literature?* Bloomington and London: Indiana University Press, 1978.

Hirsch, E. D., Jr. *The Aims of Interpretation*. Chicago: University of Chicago Press, 1976.

_____. *Validity in Interpretation*. New Haven, Conn., and London: Yale University Press, 1967.

Holland, Norman N. *The Dynamics of Literary Response*. New York and London: W. W. Norton, 1968.

_____. *Five Readers Reading*. New Haven, Conn.: Yale University Press, 1975.

_____. "A Transactive Account of Transactive Criticism." *Poetics* 7 (1978): 177–89.

Hormann, H. "The Concept of Sense Constancy." Bochum: Universität Bochum, 1975. Mimeo.

Ingarden, Roman. *The Cognition of the Literary Work of Art*. Eng. trans. Ruth Ann Crowley and Kenneth R. Olson. Northwestern Studies in Phenomenology and Existential Philosophy. Evanston, Ill.: Northwestern University Press, 1973.

_____. *The Literary Work of Art: An Investigation on the Borderlines of Ontology, Logic, and Theory of Literature*. Eng. trans. George G. Grabowicz. Northwestern Studies in Phenomenology and Existential Philosophy. Evanston, Ill.: Northwestern University Press, 1973.

Iser, Wolfgang. *The Act of Reading: A Theory of Aesthetic Response*. London and Henley: Routledge & Kegan Paul, 1978.

_____. "Indeterminacy and the Reader's Response in Prose Fiction." In *Aspects of Narrative: Selected Papers from the English Institute*, ed. J. Hillis Miller, 1–45. New York and London: Columbia University Press, 1971.

_____. "Interview." *Diacritics* 10 (1980): 57–74.

_____. "The Reading Process: A Phenomenological Approach." In *Reader-Response Criticism: From Formalism to Post-Structuralism*, ed. Jane P. Tompkins, 274–94. Baltimore and London: Johns Hopkins University Press, 1980. Reprinted from Wolfgang Iser, *The Implied Reader: Patterns in Communication in Prose Fiction from Bunyan to Beckett*. Baltimore: Johns Hopkins Press, 1974.

_____. "The Reality of Fiction: A Functionalist Approach to Literature." *New Literary History* 7 (1975–76): 7–38.

Jakobson, Roman. "Die neueste russische Poesie." In *Texte der Russische Formalisten,* 2:19–136. Munich: Wilhelm Fink, 1972.

Jauss, Hans Robert. "Literary History as a Challenge to Literary Theory." *New Literary History* 2 (1970–71): 7–37.

Jauss, Hans Robert, and Rien T. Segers. "An Interview with Hans Robert Jauss," trans. Timothy Bahti. *New Literary History* 11 (1979): 83–95.

_____. *Literaturgeschichte als Provokation der Literaturwissenschaft.* Constance: University of Konstanz, 1967.

_____. "Paradigmawechsel in der Literaturwissenschaft." *Linguistische Berichte* 3 (1969): 44–56.

Johnson, Barbara. *The Critical Difference: Essays in the Contemporary Rhetoric of Reading.* Baltimore: Johns Hopkins University Press, 1980.

Lentricchia, Frank. *After the New Criticism.* Chicago: University of Chicago Press, 1980.

Levin, David Michael. "Foreword." In Roman Ingarden, *The Literary Work of Art: An Investigation on the Borderlines of Ontology, Logic, and Theory of Literature,* trans. George G. Grabowicz, xv–xliv. Evanston, Ill.: Northwestern University Press, 1973.

Levin, Samuel R. "On the Progress of Structural Poetics." *Poetics* 8 (1979): 513–15.

Lévi-Strauss, Claude. *Myth and Meaning.* London and Henley: Routledge & Kegan Paul, 1978.

Lohner, Edgar. "The Intrinsic Method: Some Reconsiderations." In *The Disciplines of Criticism: Essays in Literary Theory, Interpretation, and History,* ed. Peter Demetz, Thomas Greene, and Lowry Nelson, Jr. New Haven, Conn., and London: Yale University Press, 1968.

Lotman, Jurij. *Die Analyse des Poetischen Textes.* Königstein: Scriptor Verlag, 1974. Eng. trans.: *Analysis of the Poetic Text.* Ed. and trans. D. Barton Johnson. Ann Arbor: Ardis, 1975.

_____. "The Content and Structure of the Concept of 'Literature.' " *PTL: A Journal for Descriptive Poetics and Theory of Literature* 1 (1976): 339–56.

_____. "The Future for Structural Poetics." *Poetics* 8 (1979): 501–7.

_____. "On Some Principle Difficulties in the Structural Description of a Text." *Linguistics* 12 (1974): 57–63.

_____. *The Structure of the Artistic Text.* Eng. trans. Gail Lenhoff and Ronald Vroon. Michigan Slavic Contributions 7. Ann Arbor: University of Michigan Press, 1977.

McKnight, Edgar V. *Meaning in Texts: The Historical Shaping of a Narrative Hermeneutics.* Philadelphia: Fortress Press, 1978.

Mukarovsky, Jan. *Aesthetic Function, Norm and Value as Social Facts.* Ann Arbor: Department of Slavic Languages and Literature, University of Michigan, 1970.

_____. "Art as a Semiotic Fact." In *Structure, Sign, and Function: Selected Essays by Jan Mukarovsky*, ed. and trans. John Burbank and Peter Steiner, 82–88. New Haven, Conn., and London: Yale University Press, 1978.

_____. "Intentionality and Unintentionality in Art." In *Structure, Sign, and Function: Selected Essays by Jan Mukarovsky*, ed. John Burbank and Peter Steiner, 89–128. New Haven, Conn., and London: Yale University Press, 1978.

_____. "On Structuralism." In *Structure, Sign, and Function: Selected Essays by Jan Mukarovsky*, ed. and trans. John Burbank and Peter Steiner, 3–13. New Haven, Conn., and London: Yale University Press, 1978.

Nietzsche, Friedrich. *Werke*. Ed. Karl Schlechta. 3 vols. Munich: Hanser, 1966.

Norris, Christopher. *Deconstruction: Theory and Practice*. New York and London: Methuen, 1982.

Perrin, Norman. "The Interpretation of the Gospel of Mark." *Interpretation* 30 (1976): 115–24.

Petöfi, Janos S. "A Formal Semiotic Text Theory as an Integrated Theory of Natural Language (Methodological Remarks)." In *Current Trends in Textlinguistics*, ed. Wolfgang U. Dressler, 35–46. New York and Berlin: Walter de Gruyter, 1978.

_____. "Towards an Empirically Motivated Grammatical Theory of Verbal Texts." In *Studies in Text Grammar*, ed. J. S. Petöfi and H. Rieser, 205–75. Dordrecht, Holland, and Boston: D. Reidel, 1973.

Poulet, Georges. "Criticism and the Experience of Interiority." In *Reader-Response Criticism: From Formalism to Post-Structuralism*, ed. Jane P. Tompkins, 41–49. Baltimore and London: Johns Hopkins University Press, 1980. Reprinted from *The Structuralist Controversy: The Language of Criticism and the Sciences of Man*, ed. Richard A. Macksey and Eugenio Donato. Baltimore: Johns Hopkins Press, 1972.

Propp, Vladimir. *Morphology of the Folktale*. Eng. trans. Laurence Scott. 2d ed. Austin: University of Texas Press, 1968.

Robinson, James M. "Hermeneutics Since Barth." *The New Hermeneutic. New Frontiers in Theology*, vol. 2. New York: Harper & Row, 1964.

Rousseau, J. J. *Oeuvres complètes*. Ed. by Bernard Gagnebin and Marcel Raymond. Paris: Gallimard, 1964.

Schmidt, Henry J. " 'Text-Adequate Concretizations' and Real Readers: Reception Theory and Its Applications." *New German Critique* 17 (1979): 157–69.

Schmidt, Siegfried J. *"Empirische Literaturwissenschaft* as Perspective." *Poetics* 8 (1979): 557–68.

_____. *Grundriss der Empirischen Literaturwissenschaft*, Teilband 1: *Der gesellschaftliche Handlungsbereich Literatur*. Braunschweig and Wiesbaden: Friedr. Vieweg, 1980.

_____. "On a Theoretical Basis for a Rational Science of Literature." *PTL: A Journal for Descriptive Poetics and Theory of Literature* 1 (1976): 239–64.

Sklovskij, Viktor. "Die Kunst als Verfahren." In *Texte der Russischen Formalisten,* 1:3–36. Munich: Wilhelm Fink, 1969.

Steiner, Peter. "Jan Mukarovsky's Structural Aesthetics." In *Structure, Sign, and Function: Selected Essays by Jan Mukarovsky,* ed. and trans. John Burbank and Peter Steiner, ix–xxxix. New Haven, Conn., and London: Yale University Press, 1978.

Suleiman, Susan R. "Introduction: Varieties of Audience-Oriented Criticism." In *The Reader in the Text,* ed. Susan R. Suleiman and Inge Crosman, 3–45. Princeton, N.J.: Princeton University Press, 1980.

Thorndyke, Perry W., and Frank R. Yekovich, "A Critique of Schema-based Theories of Human Story Memory." *Poetics* 9 (1980): 23–49.

Todorov, Tzvetan. *Grammaire du Décaméron.* The Hague: Mouton, 1969.

_____. "Structural Analysis of Narrative." *Novel: A Forum on Fiction* 3 (1969–70): 70–76.

Tynjanov, Jurij. "Das Literarische Faktum." In *Texte der Russischen Formalisten,* 1:392–431. Munich: Wilhelm Fink, 1969.

_____. "On Literary Evolution." In *Readings in Russian Poetics: Formalist and Structuralist Views,* ed. Ladislav Matejka and Krystyna Pomorska, 66–77. Cambridge and London: M. I. T. Press, 1971.

Vodicka, Felix. "Jungmanns Übersetzung von Chateaubriands Atala." In *Die Struktur der Literarischen Entwicklung,* ed. Jurij Striedter, 227–305. Munich: Wilhelm Fink, 1976.

_____. "Die Konkretisation des Literarischen Werks. Zur Problematik der Rezeption von Nerudas Werk." In *Die Struktur der Literarischen Entwicklung,* ed. Jurij Striedter, 87–125. Munich: Wilhelm Fink, 1976.

_____. "Die Literaturgeschichte, Ihre Probleme und Aufgaben: Ausgangspunkt und Gegenstand der Literaturgeschichte." In *Die Struktur der Literarischen Entwicklung,* ed. Jurij Striedter, 30–86. Munich: Wilhelm Fink, 1976.

_____. *Pocatky krasne prozy novoceske: Prispevek k literarnim dejinam doby Jungmannovy* ("The Beginnings of Modern Czech Prose Fiction: A Contribution to the Literary History of Jungmann's Era"). Prague: Melantrich, 1948.

Warren, Austin. "The Function of Literature." In *Theory of Literature,* by René Wellek and Austin Warren, 19–28. New York: Harcourt, Brace & Co., 1942.

Wellek, René. *Concepts of Criticism.* Ed. with an introduction by Stephen G. Nichols, Jr. New Haven, Conn., and London: Yale University Press, 1963.

Wellek, René, and Austin Warren. *Theory of Literature.* New York: Harcourt, Brace & Co., 1942.

Weinold, Götz. "The Concept of Text Processing, the Criticism of Literature and Some Uses of Literature in Education." In *The Uses of Criticism,* ed. A. D. Foulkes, 109–31. Bern and Frankfurt: Herbert Lang and Peter Lang, 1976.

Wimsatt, William K., Jr., and Cleanth Brooks. *Literary Criticism: A Short History.* New York: Alfred A. Knopf, 1957.

Index

Abrams, M. H., 2–3, 135
Adams, Marilyn Jager, 74, 135
Aeschylus, 102
Aesthetic objects, 16–17, 21–22, 26–27, 37, 80
Aesthetics: of identity and of opposition, 42–43; of reception, 75–78; of response, 78–82
Allegorical interpretation, xii–xiii, 1
Allegory, xii–xiii, 90–91
Analysis, 38–39, 41–43, 45–46, 50–51, 53, 56, 58–59, 61–66, 68–69, 85, 89, 111, 122, 130; of different planes, 38–39; paradigmatic and syntagmatic, 50–53; and synthesis, 43, 45, 56–57, 62–65, 130
Aristotle, 2, 10, 117, 135
Artificial language, 40
Artistic texts, 40–44, 46, 48; and nonartistic text, 42–43;
Augustine, xi–xiii, 132, 135
Author, 2–4, 8, 11–12, 15, 21, 31, 37, 39–40, 43–44, 59–61, 66, 83, 89, 95–96, 98–99, 101–3, 112, 118, 131–33; and analysis, 43–44;

concretization by reader, 37, 112; implied, 98, 101–3; as "speaking subject," 96, 98, 99, 132, 133; "Author's" perspective and "reader's" perspective, 42–44

Balzac, Honoré de, 57
Barthes, Roland, 56–57, 135
Bernstejn, Sergej, 16–17, 111–12, 135
Binary oppositions, 13, 51 n.1, 54–55
Blanks (gaps), 79–80
Bonn, University of, xv
Booth, Wayne C., 84, 101–103, 135
Bremond, Claude, 54–55, 135
Bultmann, Rudolf, xv, xviii n.5, 9

Catharsis, 119–20
Causality, deconstruction of, 86, 89, 126
Cause, 20, 47, 81, 86, 89, 126
Cavell, Stanley, 127
Character-types (spheres of action), 51
Chomsky, Noam, xvi, 60

143